GRAND CANYON RAILROAD

Illustrated Guidebook

ISBN 0-935810-44-7

PRIMER PUBLISHERS
5738 North Central Avenue
Phoenix, Arizona 85012
(602) 234-1574

GRAND CANYON RAILROAD

Illustrated Guidebook

by

Rudy J. Gerber

Photos by Rudy J. Gerber

Illustrations and maps by Peg Hogan

PRIMER PUBLISHERS

DEDICATION

To my children Jennifer, Krissey, and Joey Gerber.
May your trails in life be like those of the Canyon
and its railroad: uplifting even when uphill.

"*Brighter than the Rails,*
Grander than the Canyon"

THIS IS GRAND CANYON COUNTRY

John Hance, the famed Grand Canyon guide at the turn of the century, liked to tell stagecoach passengers the story of the young English preacher walking along the old stage trail to the Canyon. Too poor to pay the stage fare of $20, the young man had decided to walk to the Canyon from Flagstaff, a distance of some 80 miles through dense forest and barren desert. After two days and nights on the trail, his canteen was empty and there were but a few biscuits left in his pocket. His feet were blistered and his body in pain when Hance's stage picked him up. When asked why he pushed himself so, he replied that, money or not, he just had to see the "mighty miracle" ahead.

Though it too travels to this "mighty miracle," the Grand Canyon Railway makes no pretense of being as mighty or as miraculous. But the railroad does have a compelling and nearly miraculous story. It deals with courageous explorers, mountain men, Indians, stage coaches, pioneers, braggarts, Chinese laborers, Swedish loggers, Mexican section hands, ghost towns, and a bustling frontier. The present-day story is hardly different: there are still daring and innovative business people, creative townspeople, hard-working railroad folk, all combining their frontier energies.

And, of course, the railroad's story is about railroad things—old coaches made new, ancient steam engines,historic hotels, stations and campsites along 64 miles of scenic track unlike any other railroad in the country, the only one ever to penetrate to the heart of a national park.

If that were all, the story would be compelling enough. But there is more: the destination. The railroad's existence is testimony to the magnetism of the "mighty miracle" at the end of the rails. The building and rebuilding of the railroad say something about the English preacher's longing to reach the Canyon.

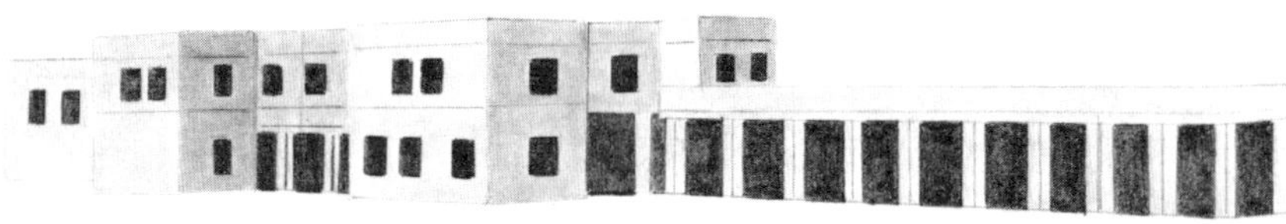

Fray Marcos Hotel and Depot in Williams shortly after its opening in 1908.

These pages describe something about making locomotives, little about making money, and much about pilgrimage. Visitors to the Canyon may not use that term for themselves or their visit. But it is not out of place in this place. Colin Fletcher, who like the English preacher felt drawn to walk to and through the Canyon, used that very term "pilgrimage" to describe his own love affair with the Canyon. In The Man Who Walked Through Time, he described his pilgrimage through the Canyon by foot as an analogue to life: plodding toward a destination that made the efforts along the way both necessary and worthwhile.

If Colin Fletcher's trip through the Canyon was a pilgrimage, the same ought to be said of those who surveyed, built, rebuilt, refurbished and traveled along the Canyon rails. The trip and its story remain a pilgrimage to all that the Canyon proclaims.

On September 17, 1989, 88 years to the day from the date the first steam engine puffed to the Grand Canyon, a reborn Grand Canyon Railway train made its way from Williams to the Grand Canyon along the same historic route.

It was a big day for the town of Williams, the Canyon, even for a good part of the southwestern United States. Some 5,000 people came to the old depot in Williams to hear the railroad praised in word and song and to wave the engine off. Several thousand more welcomed it hours later when it arrived, tired but still huffing, at the Canyon depot. Along the way, through forests and barren deserts, tracks and trees were populated with well-wishers. Red, white, and blue balloons and yellow ribbons decorated trees and right-of-way sites.

The 644 passengers on board celebrated by singing, dancing, and clapping. Two of them got married in a ceremony in the last coach car. The Governor of Arizona sent the train forth. Representatives of universities, Indian tribes, national forests, and the Grand Canyon National Park all spoke with unrestrained enthusiasm. The President of the United States and both Arizona Senators sent messages of congratulation. After all the words, champagne flowed in a christening of the old engine, and a Navajo Indian blessing wished Godspeed and safety for a long life on the rails.

The resurrection of the Grand Canyon Railway signifies more than steam and thunder, nostalgia and history. It is part of a growing recognition of the need to soften the environmental impact made by four-million annual visitors to the Canyon. The railroad uses a clean-burning fuel of oil and gray water for engine power. Eventually the trains may reduce peak motor traffic in the Canyon park by as much as 4,000 vehicles per day.

Saving the environment is enough reason for the railroad. But, thankfully, there is more. The railroad is a story of pioneer spirit, ghost towns, frontiers, mines, looming mountains, ancient seas, barren deserts, life and death, and an indomitable spirit both at the turn of the century and today.

Some general preliminary matters pertain to the entire route: -

Equipment

The railroad today includes four steam engines, each a 2-8-0 formerly used by the 103-mile Lake Superior and Ispheming (Michigan) ore-hauling railroad. Engines 18, 19, and 20 were built by American Locomotive in Pittsburgh in 1910. Number 29 came out of the same shop in 1906. All four were modernized in the late 1920s, for installation of superheaters, feedwater heaters, and thermic syphons. When these engines arrived in Williams, they were converted from coal to oil (for fire safety reasons) and had their boilers replaced. Another steam locomotive, Burlington 2-8-2 Number 4960, was purchased from Mid-Continent Railway Museum in Wisconsin.

Engines #19 and #20 sit on the tracks in Williams awaiting refurbishing. All engines were in this condition when purchased by the railroad.

Passenger coaches are 92-seat Harriman cars, built by Pullman Standard in the 1920s, which saw service as commuters on the Southern Pacific's San Francisco-San Jose route until the 1960s. These cars have been restored at either the Pacific Fruit Express car shops in Tucson or at the Grand Canyon Railway shops in Williams. Each required extensive sandblasting and repainting. The interiors are restored with green plush seats of velour and mahogany woodwork. The coaches all have concrete floors which help maintain a heavy and low center of gravity for added stability.

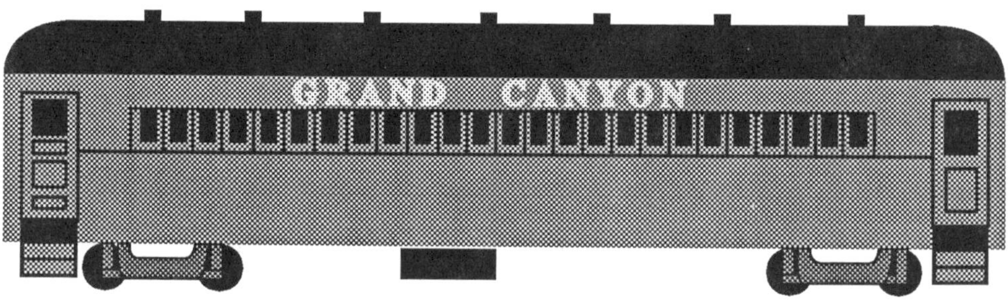

Grand Canyon Railway Harriman coach

Speeds

The lack of automatic signals under federal law restricts trains to a maximum 49 miles per hour. Practical limitations on engine number 18 (40 m.p.h. maximum) further restrict speed. Furthermore, north of Anita at milepost 45 the track becomes steep and serpentine, with a 3.22 percent grade and several horseshoe curves, followed by a steep ascent to the Canyon rim.

For all these reasons, trains on the Canyon line have never been particularly fast. The initial schedule, first published in March 1900, showed trains averaging 15 m.p.h from Williams to Anita. The following timetable for December 1911 shows a faster speed—an average of 26 m.p.h.

The Grand Canyon Railway Company

TIMETABLE NO. 29
December 10, 1911

Northward First Class 12	14		Southward First Class 11	15
Leave daily		STATIONS	Arrive daily	
PM	AM		AM	PM
1:30	5:40	WILLIAMS	10:40	10:30
1:50	6:00	PITT	10:17	9:57
1:55	6:05	RED LAKE	10:12	9:50
2:20	6:30	QUIVERO	9:47	9:27
2:37	6:47	VALLE	9:30	9:10
2:54	7:04	WILLAHA	9:13	8:53
3:12	7:23	ANITA	8:50	8:38
3:29	7:39	HOPI	8:30	8:18
3:34	7:44	APEX	8:34	8:14
3:44	7:54	COCONINO	8:28	8:08
4:00	8:10	GRAND CANYON	8:10	7:50
PM	AM		AM	PM
Arrive daily			Leave daily	

By 1961, the Santa Fe schedule announced average speeds between 24.9 and 29.7 m.p.h.

Timetable No. 4
April 30, 1961

Westward FIRST CLASS **15**		Eastward FIRST CLASS **14**
Leave daily		Leave daily
AM		**PM**
4:25	WILLIAMS	10:10
4:45	RED LAKE	9:48
5:10	QUIVERO	9:25
5:30	VALLE	9:09
5:48	WILLAHA	8:54
6:01	ANITA	8:43
6:20	APEX	8:27
6:35	COCONINO	8:15
7:00	GRAND CANYON	8:00
(24.9 mph)	Average speed per hour	(29.7 mph)

The maximum speed on the route today is about 35 m.p.h. On steep ascents and sharp curves the speed may drop to as low as 10 m.p.h. The following table may be used to determine train speeds:

TRAIN PASSES MILEPOSTS IN	TRAIN SPEED
1 minute	60 m.p.h.
2 minute	30 m.p.h.
3 minute	20 m.p.h.
4 minute	15 m.p.h.
5 minute	12 m.p.h.
6 minute	10 m.p.h.

Geology

The southern area of the route, extending roughly from Williams north to Quivero at milepost 20, is part of one of the largest volcanic fields in the United States. It is dotted with more than 400 volcanoes and cinder cones, plus lava flows and formations. Bill Williams Mountain just south of Williams is one of several mountains where light silicic volcanic rock occurs. This kind of lava squeezes up into volcanic domes. Bill Williams Mountain consists of a central cluster of spires surrounded by 12 volcanic domes. Sitgreaves and Kendricks Mountains farther east are similar, smaller centers of silicic magma. When silicic magma erupts from the same vent, a stratovolcano develops. The San Francisco Peaks near Flagstaff provide a good example.

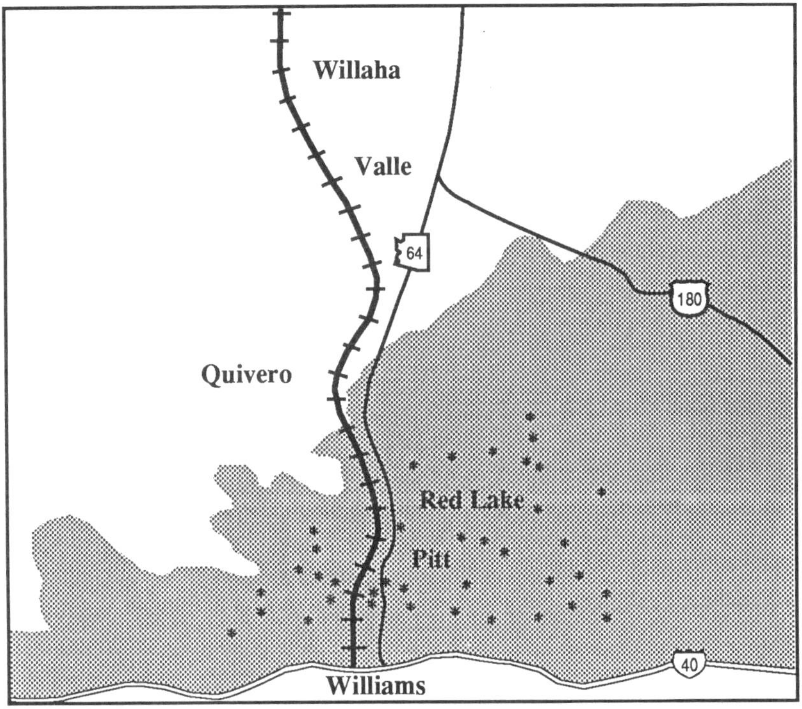

The shaded portion represents rock of volcanic origins extending from Williams almost to Quivero. The unshaded portion north all the way to the Canyon is Kaibab limestone. Asterisks indicate major volcanoes.

The volcanic peaks become younger as one moves from west to east. Bill Williams Mountain dates from about four million years ago, whereas Sitgreaves and Kendricks erupted less than two million years ago. Humphrey's Peak in the San Francisco Mountain range northwest of Flagstaff was formed between 200,000 and one million years ago. Sunset Crater just east of Flagstaff probably erupted about A.D. 1250. Thus the older, more rounded volcanic formations cluster along the rails, whereas the younger, more sharply defined formations lie farther east toward Flagstaff.

The Roadbed

The Canyon railway was first graded north from Williams in June 1899. By early 1900 the track was laid to within 11 miles of the Canyon. After a delay caused by financial reorganization, the tracks were eventually completed to the rim in 1901, with the first train arriving September 17.

The roadbed runs along a gently rolling countryside generally shaped like a bowl, with the highest areas at the southern and northern ends. The southern end near Williams is high because of hundreds of feet of volcanic cinder sitting atop buried limestone. About twenty miles north of Williams, the tracks begin to cross a sloping depression. This area was worn smooth by winds, erosion and, most importantly, by the undulating action of successive saltwater seas. The northern end, topped with stratified limestone, slopes upward to the Canyon rim.

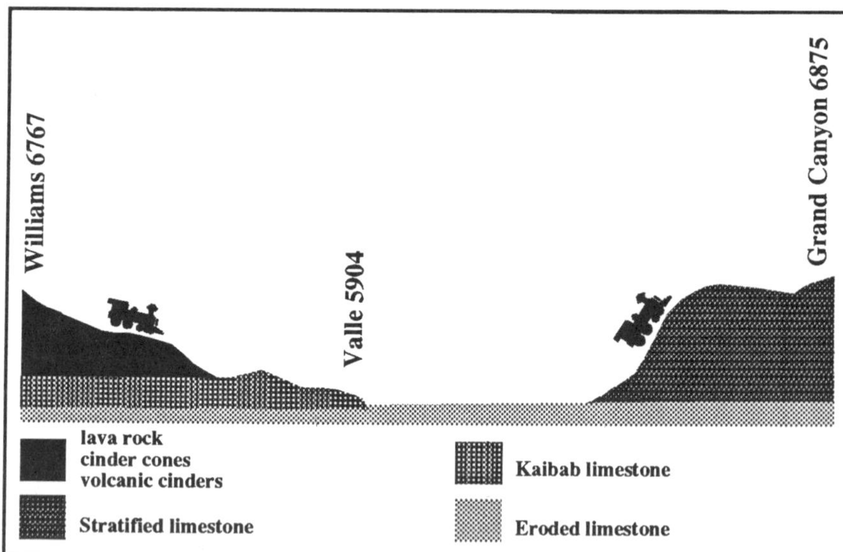

Elevations along the railroad line from Williams to the Grand Canyon.

The ballast for the roadbed is taken from volcanic cinder pits along the route, notably near mileposts 6, 7, and 8. An area near milepost 8 is used to store and load cinder onto gondola cars for ballasting the entire line. Cinder is soft yet stable. Unlike other roadbeds, it has the added advantage of allowing exceptional drainage. That, coupled with the dry climate, permits the crossties a long decay-free life.

The main line is essentially a due-north course of 64 miles with original spur roadbeds at Pitt, Anita, Apex, and turnaround wyes at the Canyon and Williams. All these side tracks have been removed with the exception of the wyes at the Canyon and Williams. The roadbeds, however, are still visible in many places. Many of the original ties remain in place, particularly in the 2.87 mile spur which ran to the ore mines northeast of Anita. The wye and spur at Apex were originally built to serve logging interests. The spur has been removed but is intended to be rebuilt four miles farther east to service the Grand

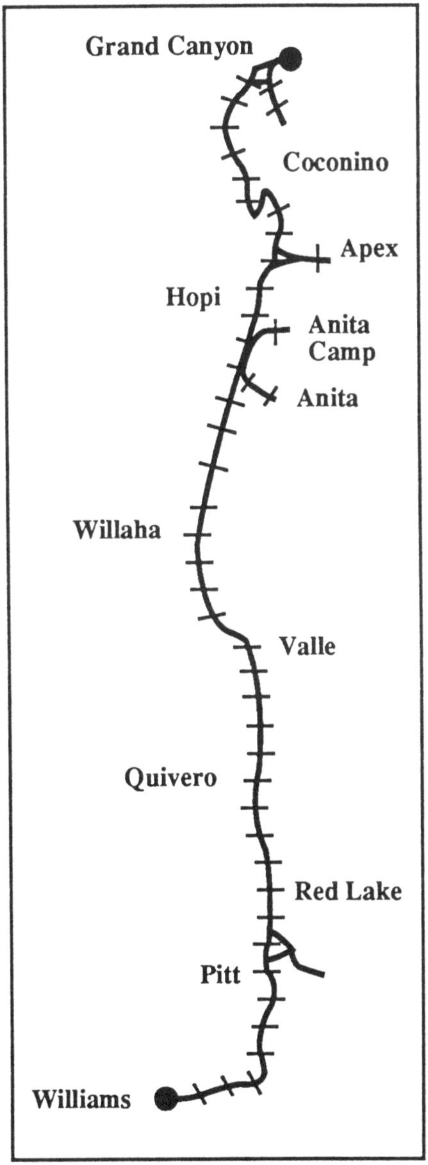

Spur lines and wyes circa 1930.

Canyon Airport so air passengers can leave the terminal and take a train directly to the Canyon rim. The 112-pound jointed rails are maintained to Federal Railroad Administration (FRA) Class 3 standards which permit speeds up to 60 m.p.h.

Life Zones

"Life zones" are terms coined by biologist Charles Merriam who did research in 1889 in the rectangle formed by the Grand Canyon, Williams, and Flagstaff. Merriam identified the balance between climate and altitude achieved by plants and animals. Flowers that are found growing at the top of 12,630 ft. Humphrey's Peak north of Flagstaff also appear in the arctic circle in northern Greenland.

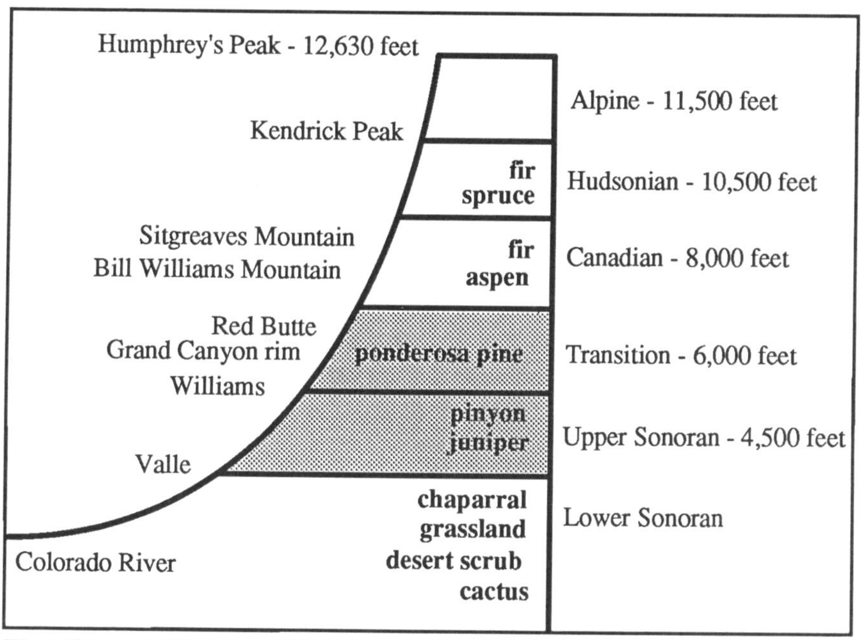

Elevation and life zones visible from the Canyon railroad with representative trees and vegetation illustrating each zone. The railroad traverses the Upper Sonoran and the Transition life zones.

Merriam's research in the area near the Canyon railroad has permitted insights into plant and animal classification by climatic zones. Arranged from lowest elevation to highest, the five life zones are: Lower Sonoran (named after the Sonoran Desert) which exhibits sea level and desert life; Upper Sonoran, beginning about 4,500 feet, with piñon pine, juniper, and chaparral; Transition, beginning at 6,000 feet, characterized by ponderosa pine; Canadian, at 8,000 feet, with fir and aspen; Hudsonian, at 10,500 feet, with fir and spruce; and, at the highest elevation, the Alpine life zone, beginning about 11,500 feet, characterized by the absence of trees and the presence of small, delicate and usually stemless plants.

The route of the Canyon railroad traverses two of these life zones - the Upper Sonoran and the Transition. From the train windows the careful observer can see the higher life zones on the larger mountains to the east of the rails, particularly Sitgreaves, Kendrick, and Humphrey's Peaks.

Wildlife

Elk and deer are often seen in the piñon and ponderosa forests adjoining the tracks. Mule deer are prevalent in the Williams area, although whitetails are occasionally seen. The differences between the two are apparent as they run away: the whitetail runs in long leaps which show the large, white underside of its tail. The mule deer, on the other hand, bounds away as if on a pogo stick without revealing the underside of its tail.

Mule deer are found in all parts of the Kaibab Forest north of Williams and near the Canyon. Whitetail deer tend to be more prevalent in the southern part of the Kaibab.

The sight of a mature elk is awesome. The male's weight varies from 700 to 1,000 pounds and a mature cow weighs about 500 pounds. The original elk in Arizona was Merriam's Elk, which was reduced to extinction by hunting. The elk now here were transplanted from the northern Rocky Mountain states. These animals are found in all areas of the Williams district of the Kaibab Forest. Elk were first transplanted to the Coconino Plateau north of Williams near Valle. They have gradually migrated to the pine-covered areas north and south.

The primary summer habitats for elk are ponderosa pine forests. In the winter they are found in lower elevations of piñon and juniper forests where grasses and forbs are available. They can be seen along the edges of groves of trees.

"Leave it as it is. You cannot improve on it. The ages have been at work on it, and man can only mar it. What you can do is to keep it for your children, your children's children, and for all who come after you, as the one great sight which every American ... should see." – President Theodore Roosevelt, speaking of the Grand Canyon, May 1903.

MILE BY MILE GUIDE

The following pages describe historic and scenic areas along the railroad right of way between Williams and the Canyon. The description follows the sequence of mileposts along the tracks beginning at the station in Williams. Mileposts are located near the tracks. Most of them are on the east side of the rails. They face in both directions. Northbound passengers may use this guide in the sequence printed here; southbound passengers should begin with the account at milepost 64 and read toward the lower-numbered mileposts. As you read, refer to the detailed milepost maps throughout this section. A complete two-page map is in the center of the book.

Mile 0: Williams, Arizona. Trains arrive and depart on the south side of the original Santa Fe station adjoining the historic Fray Marcos Hotel. The entire structure is built of poured concrete. It opened in 1908. It is named after Marcos de Niza, the Franciscan friar who journeyed through this area to the Canyon in 1540 as chaplain and pathfinder for the Coronado expedition searching for the fabled seven golden cities of Cibola.

On the station's wall hangs the official elevation marker for Williams showing its elevation as 6,767 feet above sea level. Bill Williams Mountain, named for the legendary mountain man and guide, rises to 9,256 feet directly south of town. The mountain marks the western boundary of the lands inhabited by the Hopi Indians, who view both this mountain and the San Francisco peaks cluster to the east as sacred.

Statue of Bill Williams at the west end of the town named after him.

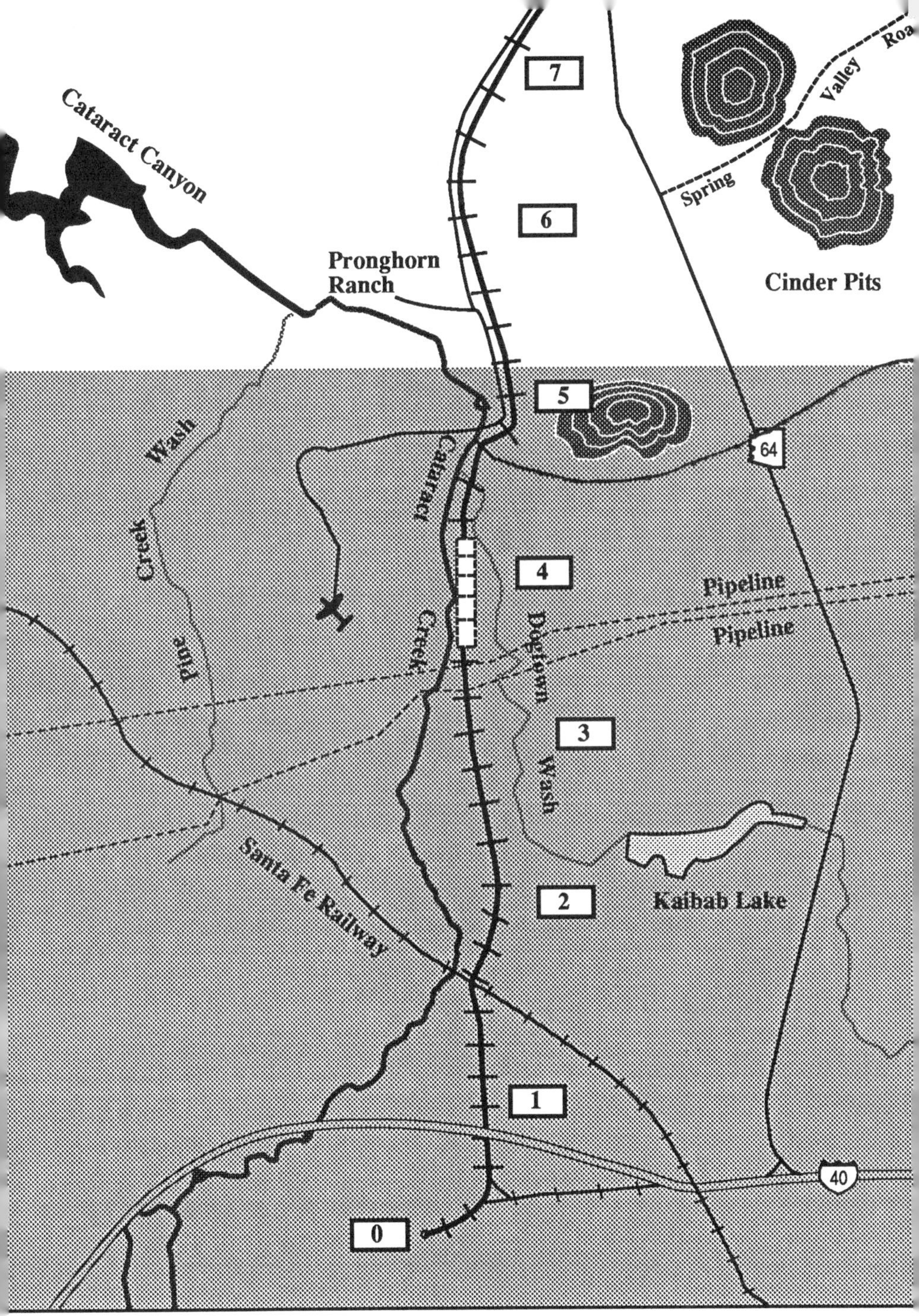

Cataract Canyon
Pronghorn Ranch
7
6
5
4
3
2
1
0
Spring Valley Road
Cinder Pits
64
Pine Creek Wash
Cataract Creek
Dogtown Wash
Pipeline
Pipeline
Santa Fe Railway
Kaibab Lake
40

Milepost 0-7

The name Williams was given to the mountain and the stream in the area as early as 1852 by the Sitgreaves expedition, but other names were used for the town. In the early 1870s, Charles F. Rogers built and lived in a large cabin here. When wagon freighters came, Mrs. Rogers gave them lodging and meals and the place became known as "Roger's Stop", and soon became a regular haven for travelers, thanks to Mrs. Rogers's cooking. Droughts of the 1870s drove many cattle and sheep to this spot, giving rise to early ranching. The area then was primarily marshland. In the 1870s it was known to the Indians as "Jock-Ha-We-Hah" or "covered with evergreens."

To provide ties for the railroad, logging camps were established at Chalender and Sun Up two miles west of Roger's Stop. In 1881 railroad graders arrived. Mr. Rogers had his place designated a post office and suggested the name "Williams" after Bill Williams and his mountain. As only Williams had water, the railroad located its shops here. Soon the residents of Sun Up moved their town bodily into Williams.

From 1882 to 1890 the livestock business flourished: 200 people lived in the central part of town and more than 300 cowboys lived on nearby ranges. A school and church were first built in 1891. The Saginaw Lumber Company began in 1892 and was succeeded by the Saginaw and Manistee Lumber Company in 1899, which eventually did major lumbering operations at milepost 52 near Apex. The population of the Williams area now is approximately 3,000.

Milepost 1: Trains departing Williams leave the yards, turn north and pass Grand Canyon Railway service buildings and a diesel fuel tank on the east, cross under Interstate 40 and then under the Santa Fe east-west mainline. Amtrak's Southwest Chief passes here daily. Connections to Amtrak trains can be made at Flagstaff.

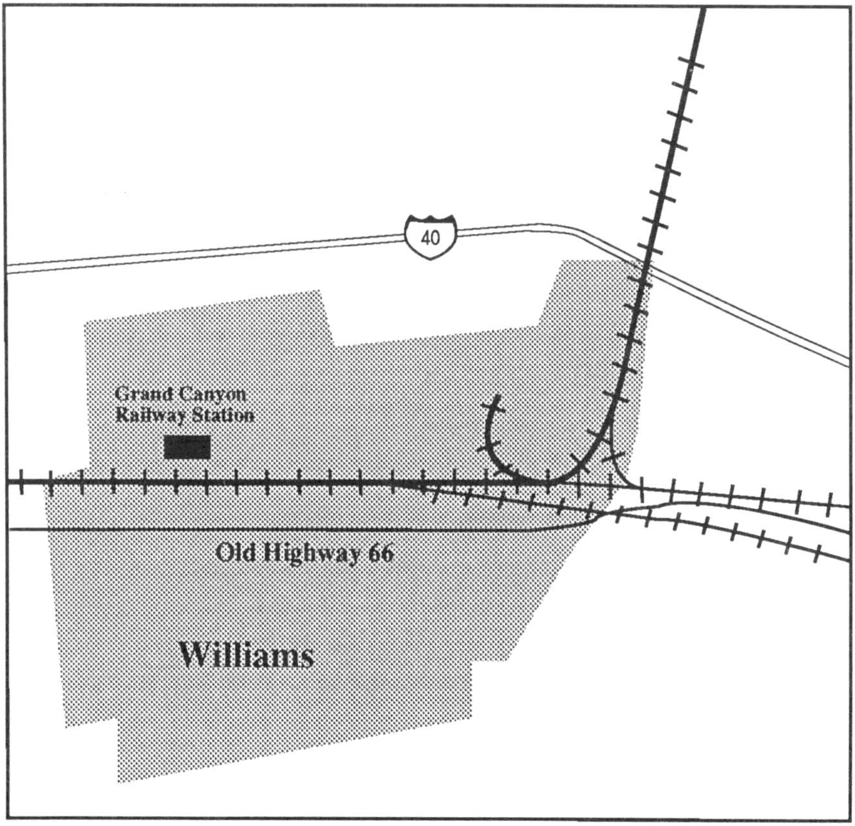

<u>Mile 1.5</u>: Trains enter the Kaibab National Forest at this point. Dude Mountain lies several miles to the east. Three Sisters Mountain with its distinctive humps is on the west, with Hearst Mountain farther west. North of the I-40 underpass, Lake Ellen is east and the Williams water treatment facilities lie on the west side of the tracks.

Milepost 2: Northbound trains enter dense ponderosa pine forests. Gonzales Lake–part of the former Gonzales ranch–is to the west of the tracks.

Dogtown Wash cuts deeply along the east side of the tracks. Kaibab Lake, one of several large snow-fed reservoirs providing water for Williams, lies east of the tracks through ponderosa pine trees. The lake is at the base of the three-humped mountain to the northeast. Forest service campgrounds are on the south shore, a pumphouse is visible briefly under the trees to the east.

Milepost 3: Williams City Airport, elevation 6,563 feet, lies west of the tracks atop the small rise on the immediate horizon. Charles Lindbergh selected its site in 1928. Three Mile Lake, named for milepost 3, lies just south of the airport. The cleared areas on each side of the roadbed mark underground natural gas pipelines which cross beneath the tracks.

Milepost 4: Dogtown Wash joins Cataract Creek. The bridge here at 182 feet is the longest on the line. High water at this location has caused occasional problems both for stagecoaches and trains. A fatal accident occurred here on September 20, 1902, because of a derailment as the roadbed was being refurbished by a work train.

Innocent-looking at this point, Cataract Creek eventually becomes the largest stream from the south feeding into the Colorado River deep in the Canyon. Francisco Garces, a Franciscan priest, and his expedition visited this area on June 19, 1776, camped here and named this creek "Rio Jabesua de San Antonio."

Mile 4.5: Just north of the cattle guard, Pronghorn Ranch Road crosses the tracks. It is named for the antelope species common in this area which, like deer, cattle, and sheep, can be seen alongside the tracks. Immediately east of the tracks are volcanic mountains whose cinders are being mined. "Prairie Dog" cinder mine lies just east of the tracks. A state-owned gravel pit, not volcanic, is on the west side of the tracks.

Crossing Pronghorn Ranch Road, southbound trains enter and northbound trains leave the Kaibab National Forest. Northbound trains will re-enter the forest near milepost 45.

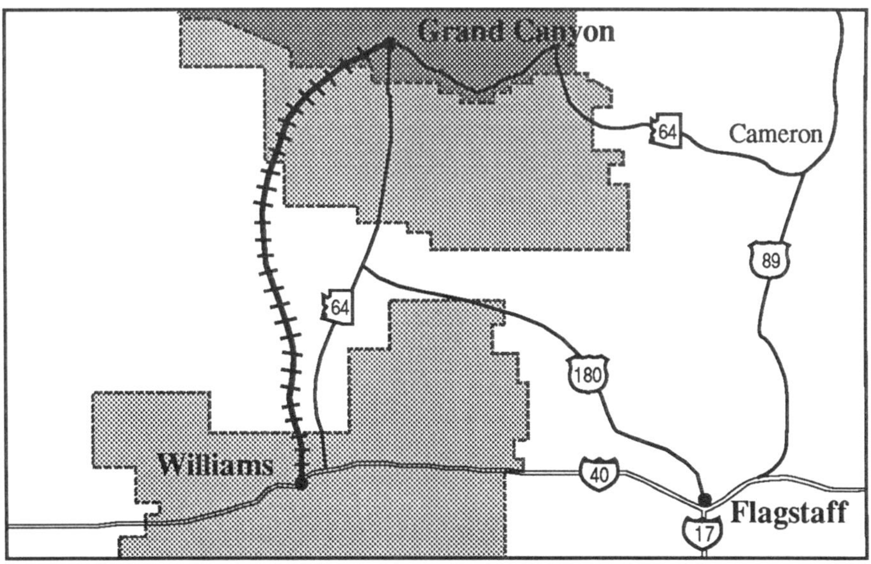

Kaibab National Forest   Grand Canyon National Park

Milepost 6: "Pitt," elevation 6,542 feet, was the site of a loading station and housing for a railroad section crew which once worked the volcanic cinder pit visible east of the tracks. The name derives either from this pit or from William Pitt, a local sheepherder living here in the late 1800s. In 1920 the section gang moved to Williams and these quarters were abandoned. The concrete remains of the bunkhouse and cistern are visible under scrub juniper trees east of the roadbed.

Mile 6.5: A wye (pronounced as the letter "Y", whose shape it resembles) existed here from the first days of the railroad, its southern leg connecting the mainline at mile 6.5 and its northern leg at milepost 7. The wye served not only as a turn-around but also as access to the volcanic cinder pit visible in the double-peaked mountain directly east of the tracks where Spring Valley Road meets Highway 64.

The cinder pit appears as the large grey gash on the southwestern face of the twin cones immediately northeast of milepost 6. The roadbed of the original wye leading to the pit can still be seen. Some of the original ties are still in place. The black and red cinders of the wye roadbed arc east and south from the mainline, cross Highway 64 and ascend the mountain.

The Santa Fe acquired rights to these cinders by court action at the turn of the century. In early construction days Chinese laborers using hand shovels dug cinders from this pit and loaded them into gondola cars. The cinders furnished ballast for the entire line during its construction and are still used for that purpose today.

At miles 6-7 southbound passengers have good views of Williams Mountain, Hearst Mountain and Three Sisters Mountain directly ahead of the train.

Milepost 7: The northern leg of the wye described just above formerly joined the mainline here. The old cinder roadbed can be seen curving southeast from milepost sign 7.

The Santa Fe was especially proud of its volcanic cinder roadbed. The railroad considered these cinders proof of the smoothness of its line. A 1903 Santa Fe brochure proclaimed:

"*The railroad track to the canyon is remarkably smooth for a new line. It is built across a slightly rolling mesa, in places thickly wooded, in others open. The snow-covered San Francisco Peaks are on the eastern horizon. Kendricks, Sitgreaves, and Williams mountains are also visible. Red Butte, thirty miles distant, is a prominent local landmark.... The route here is amid fragrant pines, over low hills and along occasional gulches and washes. Taken under the favorable conditions which generally prevail at this high altitude, the journey is a novelty and a delight.*"

Milepost 8: Espee Road crosses the tracks. A cinder loading and parking area adjoins the track on the east. This area is used to screen and load volcanic cinders onto gondola cars, as was done for roadbed reconstruction in the summer of 1989.

Sitgreaves Mountain, elevation 9,388 feet, with its camel-like rounded humps, is visible periodically to the east between mileposts 5 and 9. Its origins are volcanic. The mountain is named after Captain Lorenzo Sitgreaves, who led a U. S. Army expedition through this area to establish a westward route from Santa Fe to California. Cone-headed

Kendrick Mountain, elevation 10,418 feet, rises farther to the northeast. It is named after Sitgreaves's military escort. The mountain sits in the Kendrick Wilderness area, one of two pristine wilderness areas within the Kaibab National Forest. On its crown is a fire lookout. Four separate lava flows created Kendrick Mountain. Erosion has lowered the top of Kendrick Mountain by 1,000 feet and carved three canyons prominent in its sides.

MILEPOST 9: The tiny village of Red Lake, elevation 6,263 feet, lies immediately east along Highway 64. The community is named for the small volcanic lake directly east of milepost 9. The lake becomes red after rainfall because of red cinders in its banks and bottom. Loading pens for cattle existed here from the early days of the railroad, along with a 31-car siding for cattle cars. A post office was located in Red Lake from June 1898 to September 1899 during railroad construction. A telegraph station operated here at the turn of the century as well. Recently, Red Lake has become an art center where artists produce and sell wood, stone and other western craft.

Mile 9.5: Red Lake Wash runs along the west side of the roadbed and crosses under the tracks near Red Lake.

Milepost 10: Cedar Mountain, elevation 7,725 feet, another volcanic peak, is the dominant sight to the east of the tracks. A road leads to a cave at its top. Its heights are dotted not with cedars but with junipers.

Mile 10.5: Also of volcanic origin, Wildcat Hill well to the east has a lava cave near its top large enough for human entry. Northbound trains now begin to pull away from Highway 64; southbound trains approach it.

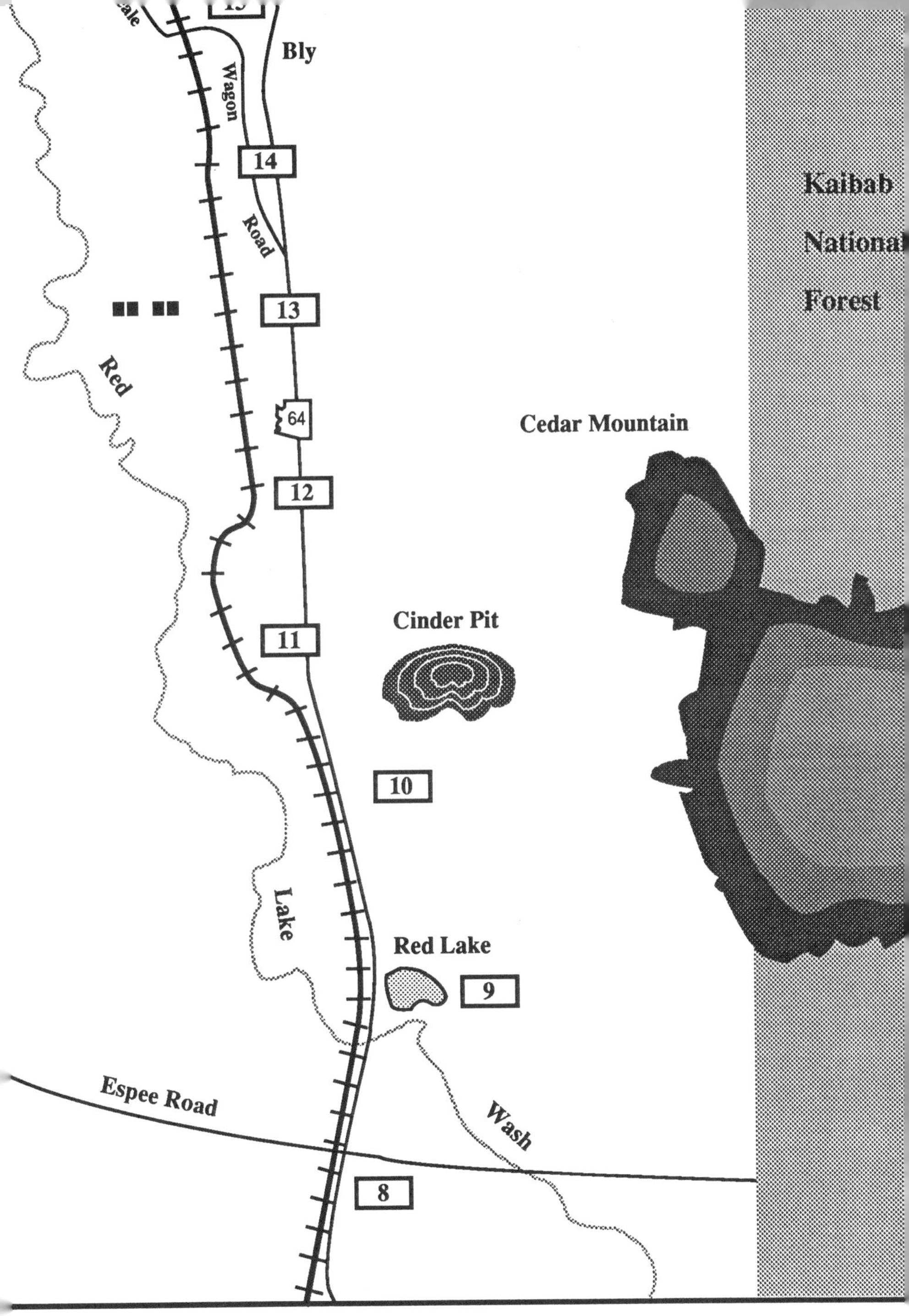

Milepost 8-15

Milepost 11-12: Squaw Mountain, elevation 7,942 feet, lies northeast of Cedar Mountain in piñon and juniper groves.

Milepost 13: Cattle pens west of the tracks are still in use. The Kaibab Forest boundary parallels the tracks farther to the east. Laws Spring, not visible from the tracks, lies several miles directly east. The Beale expedition camped here in 1857.

Edward "Ned" Beale had the task in 1857 to survey and make a western wagon road almost a third of the way across the nation. He knew that his road would serve as a preliminary approximation for a western railroad from the midwest to the Pacific coast. He was also testing a curious experiment of Jefferson Davis: to see if camels could become as useful and popular as horses as beasts of burden.

The army purchased camels, hired Arabian camel drivers and shipped them all to Texas. From there they joined Beale's party in New Mexico. In mid-1857 Beale lined up his men and camels ("lovable and docile" he called them) and began to plod westward along the 35th parallel. His caravan consisted of 22 camels, eight wagons, two "ambulances" loaded with surveying equipment, and a herd of 350 sheep and 56 men. By September 11, 1857, he was at the base of the San Francisco Peaks which, he noted, "look down frowning on us." He moved westward across Government Prairie north of Williams. His careful diary shows his enthusiasm for the country:

"Leaving breakfast camp, we traveled rapidly over a lovely country of open forest and mountain valley, which continually drew exclamations of delight and surprise from every member of the party."

Beale traveled northwest over Spring Valley and north of the town of Williams about 15 miles above its present location. For a mile and a half his road coincides with the railroad.

The area around Laws Spring is triply historic. Petroglyphs on the boulders around the spring have been traced to Cohonino Indians roaming the area from A.D. 700 to 1100. Members of Beale's expedition camped at the spring in 1857 on their first westward effort and added their own inscriptions. In April 1868, a Union Pacific Railroad survey crew contemplating a route through northern Arizona camped here and added further inscriptions to the boulders.

To the east of Laws Spring lie other memorials to Beale's wagon road: Beale Flat, Beale Mountain, and Beale Tank.

<u>Milepost 14</u>: Beale Wagon Road runs parallel to the tracks through juniper and piñon trees on the east, meets the tracks here and follows the roadbed for another mile before turning due west. The wagon road was built between 1857-1859 to link the Santa Fe Trail to the west coast. The Santa Fe Railroad, Route 66, and present-day Interstate 40, all roughly follow Beale's routing.

Red Lake Wash runs west of the tracks here. Its water flows northwest to Cataract Canyon. High voltage transmission lines cross diagonally overhead.

<u>Mile 14.9</u>: Bly, elevation 6,149 feet. The name comes from the Fletcher Bly Sheep ranch extending north from Williams. There was a small station here with a nine-car spur track for loading cattle and sheep. Limestone now begins to appear intermittently between Bly and Quivero at milepost 20,

where it becomes dominant. Between mileposts 14 and 20 it is interspersed with volcanic lava. Limestone, unlike lava, is a soft, sedimentary rock formed in marine rather than fresh waters. Like salt and gypsum it may be precipitated from an evaporating sea, as probably occurred in the area between Quivero and Anita long ago. The nucleus for most of this limestone is calcium carbonate in the form of shells which accumulated on the ancient sea floor in great abundance. In some cases the original shells in this limestone can be recognized. In most cases waves, wind, and attrition have destroyed the organic structures.

Milepost 15-16: Smoot Lake lies over a small ridge east of the tracks. It is named for William H. Smoot, a cattleman living in the area about 1881. Cattle pens are still in use on the west. Two old pioneer cabins, now abandoned, sit to the east.

Milepost 17: Howard Lake and Howard Mesa lie over a ridge several miles to the east. Their names probably derive from Charles E. Howard, owner of the Howard Sheep Company. Or possibly from Jesse Jefferson Howard, known as "Bear Howard", a local mountain man who made it his life's work to hunt bear after one killed his partner in this area in the 1880s.

Buck Mountain, elevation 7,454 feet, rises to the east. Like other mountains in the area, its origins are volcanic.

Milepost 20: Quivero, elevation 6,035 feet. The name most likely comes from "Quivera," one of the seven fabled cities of gold sought by the Coronado Expedition which passed near here in 1540 under the lead of Don Garcia Lopez de Cardenas. This expedition made the white man's first discovery of the Grand Canyon, bequeathing names for El Tovar

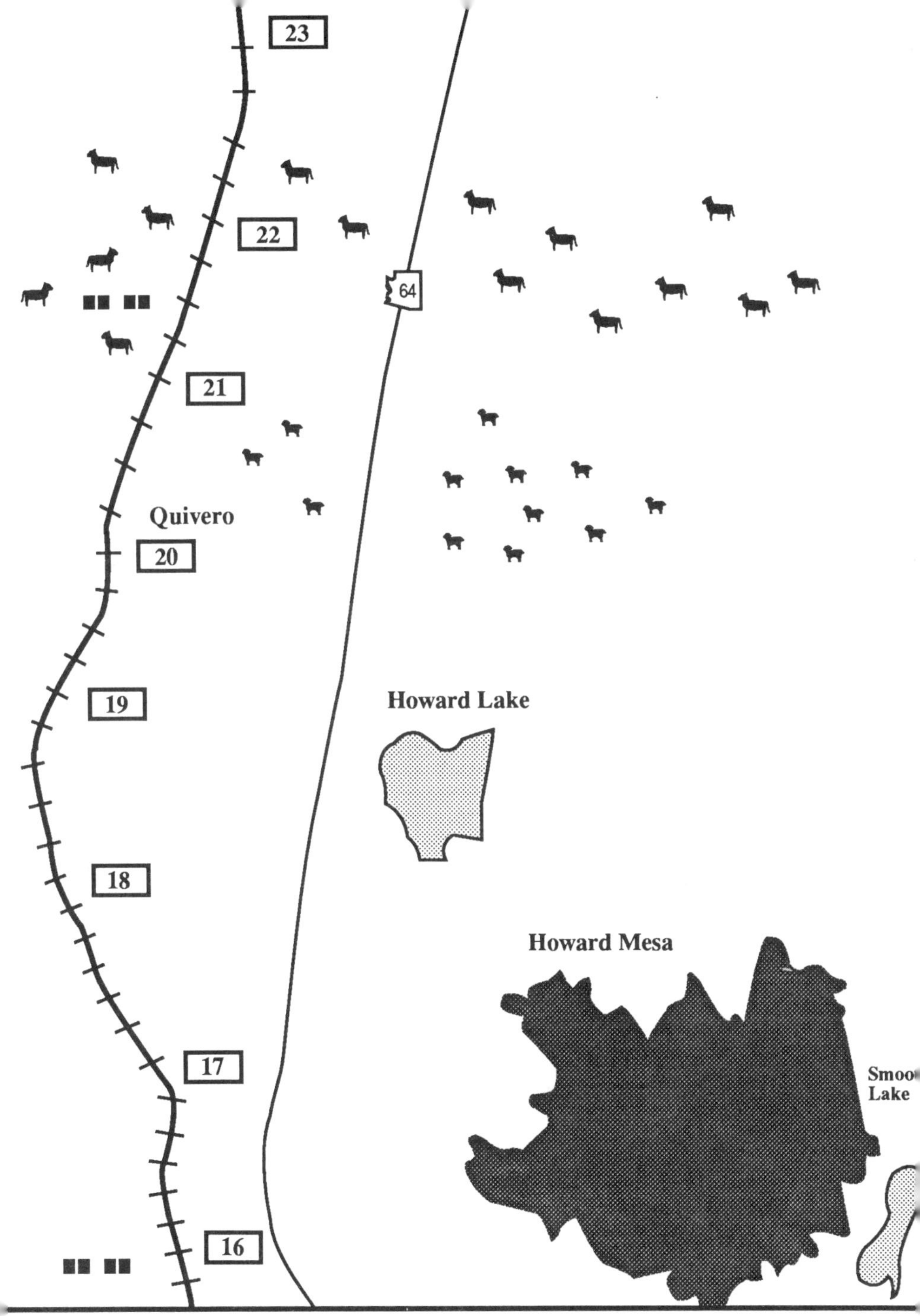

Milepost 16-23

Hotel at the Grand Canyon and for the Fray Marcos depot in Williams. Although there is no known gold in the area, there are intermittent copper deposits here which could account for the name and the illusion of gold.

In its heyday Quivero was a large sheep shipment area. Cattle and sheep pens are on the west of the tracks. Ruins of the old station are to the east. The last sheep shipment by rail left here October 10, 1972.

Beginning near Quivero at milepost 20 the entire surface is Kaibab limestone, which constitutes almost all the Coconino Plateau. This limestone rises gradually northward to the rim of the Canyon and is trenched at intervals by washes opening westward and draining into Cataract Creek, which flows into the Canyon to the northwest. In this region the plateau does not produce the pine, juniper or piñon forests characteristic of the north and south ends.

Milepost 22: Red Hill, another volcanic peak, rises several miles to the east. This area, like much of the land between Williams and the Canyon, is open range. This means that both wild and domestic animals have the right of way. Often they loiter on the track and refuse to move. Sometimes in the past the trains could not stop in time. Nimble deer and antelope were rarely a problem, but sheep, cattle and wild burros were often inspired by curiosity not to move. In a collision sheep caused the greatest problem because wool and tallow would ball up under the wheels, foul air lines to the brakes, and make it difficult to stop.

Milepost 29: Valle, elevation 5,904 feet, is the name given this small settlement of ranching buildings on both sides

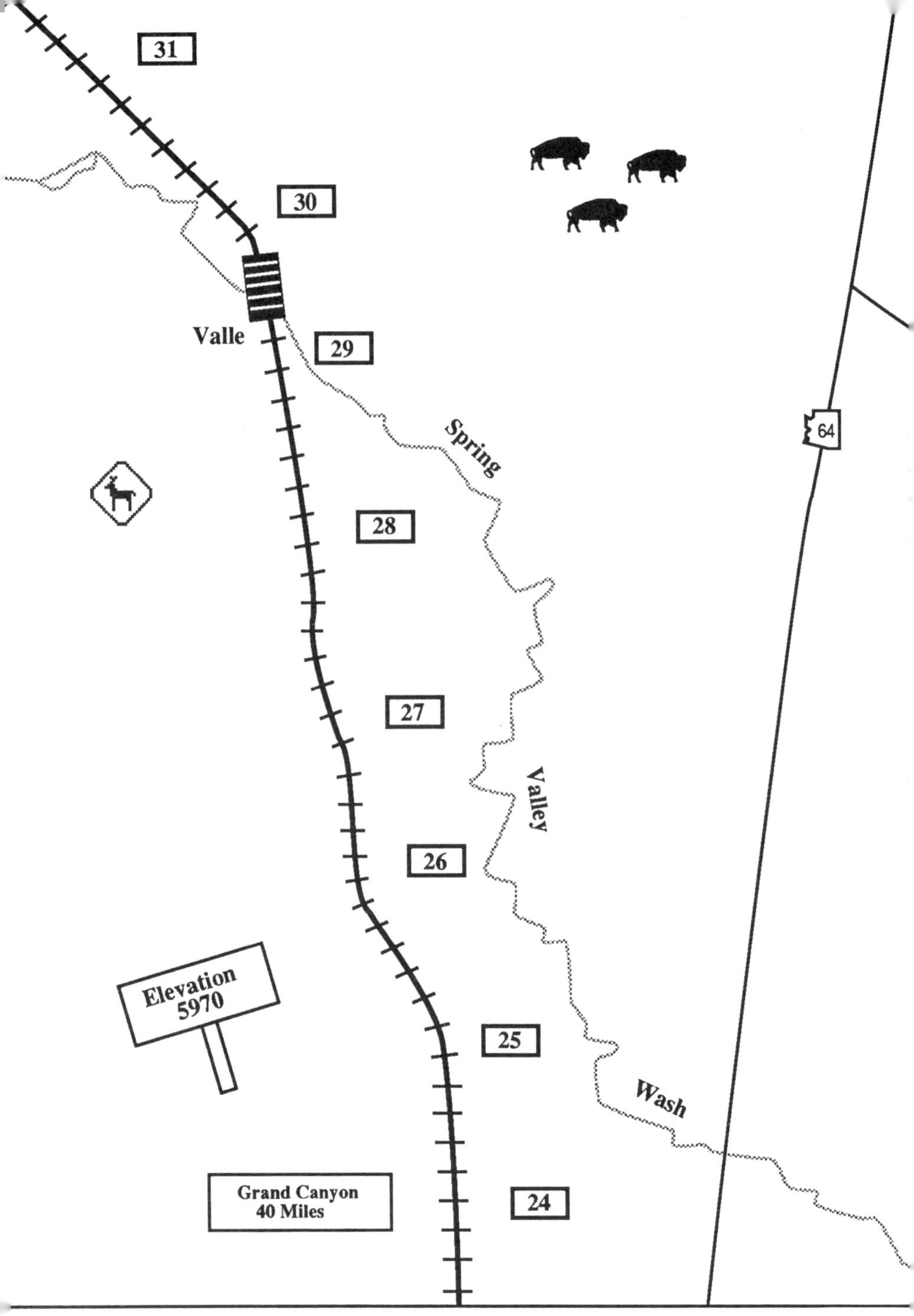

Milepost 24-31

of the tracks. The name derives from the Spanish word for valley, an appropriate description for the level and barren area where Spring Valley Wash again cuts deeply under the trestle.

Valle lies at the center of the Coconino Plateau, a large bowl-shaped depression bordered on the south by the Mogollon Rim, on the west by Aubrey Cliffs, on the north by the Grand Canyon and on the east by Grey Mountain.

On the west are concrete remains of the small station existing here from the early days of the railroad, along with a former 37-car siding serving the loading pens visible from the tracks. The masonry bridge here is 118 feet long; at 50 feet, it is the highest bridge on the line. In the railroad's early days the Grand Canyon Sheep Company used this area for loading sheep and cattle onto southbound trains to Williams. The area is still used for cattle and sheep grazing.

Milepost 30-31: The train now heads toward the lowest point of a wide, barren depression which 200 million years ago, in the Permian period, was a vast saltwater sea extending from the Canyon area southward past where Flagstaff now sits. Coral and shark relics have been found in this area, particularly in the limestone cliffs farther north. The salt left by this sea may account for the sparse vegetation.

The sea receded and then returned a second time, its shores lapping against the limestone cliffs near the Canyon on the north, the peaks to the east and the south, and the Aubrey Cliffs far to the west. The major washes that cut through the seabed and pass under the tracks—Spring Valley, Red Lake, Miller, Red Horse, Rain Tank, and Coconino—all helped feed this sea long ago and also helped to drain it.

One notes the absence of any sharply defined geological features; the rocks, mounds, and elevations in the area have been rounded by centuries of erosion and caressing waters. The elevation here is 5,800 feet, the lowest of the entire line, some 1,000 feet below Williams and the Canyon. Precipitation is infrequent. Ponderosa pine and piñon, which could grow at this elevation, are absent. The sole vegetation consists of sagebrush, greasewood, and gamma grass.

Milepost 32: Antelope are often seen in this open range area. Unlike most other animals, they have no fear of the open. Antelope are rarely seen close up because they have exceptional eyesight and sustained high-speed running ability. They can best be seen from a distance with binoculars.

Bucks have forked horns which extend well beyond the ears in mature animals. The outer sheath is shed annually. The doe sometimes has horns but these seldom extend beyond the ears. The major food sources for antelope are forbs and grass.

Young antelope are often born as twins in late May or June. After three or four days they can outrun a human being and at one week they can run for a period as fast as mature antelope. Pronghorn antelope, native to this area, are the fastest animals in North America. They have been clocked at speeds up to 60 m.p.h.

Most of the antelope in the Canyon-Williams-Flagstaff rectangle are found in open areas such as those near Valle or along pipeline right-of-ways which cross the tracks.

Mileposts 33: Southbound passengers have good views of Sitgreaves and Kendricks Mountains to the southeast. These mountains are described in the text adjoining milepost 8.

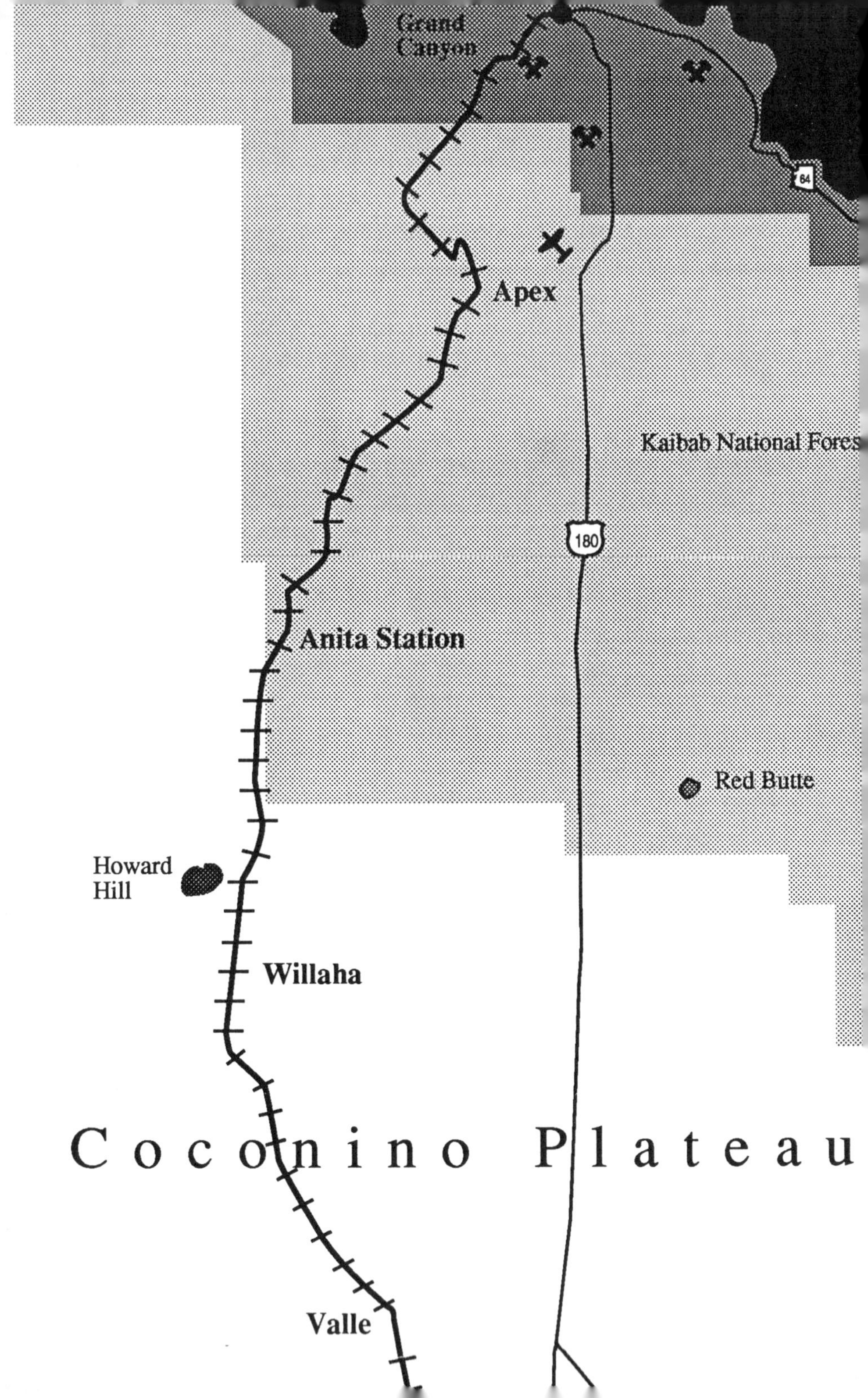
Grand
Canyon
64
Apex
Kaibab National Fores
180
Anita Station
Red Butte
Howard
Hill
Willaha
Coconino Plateau
Valle

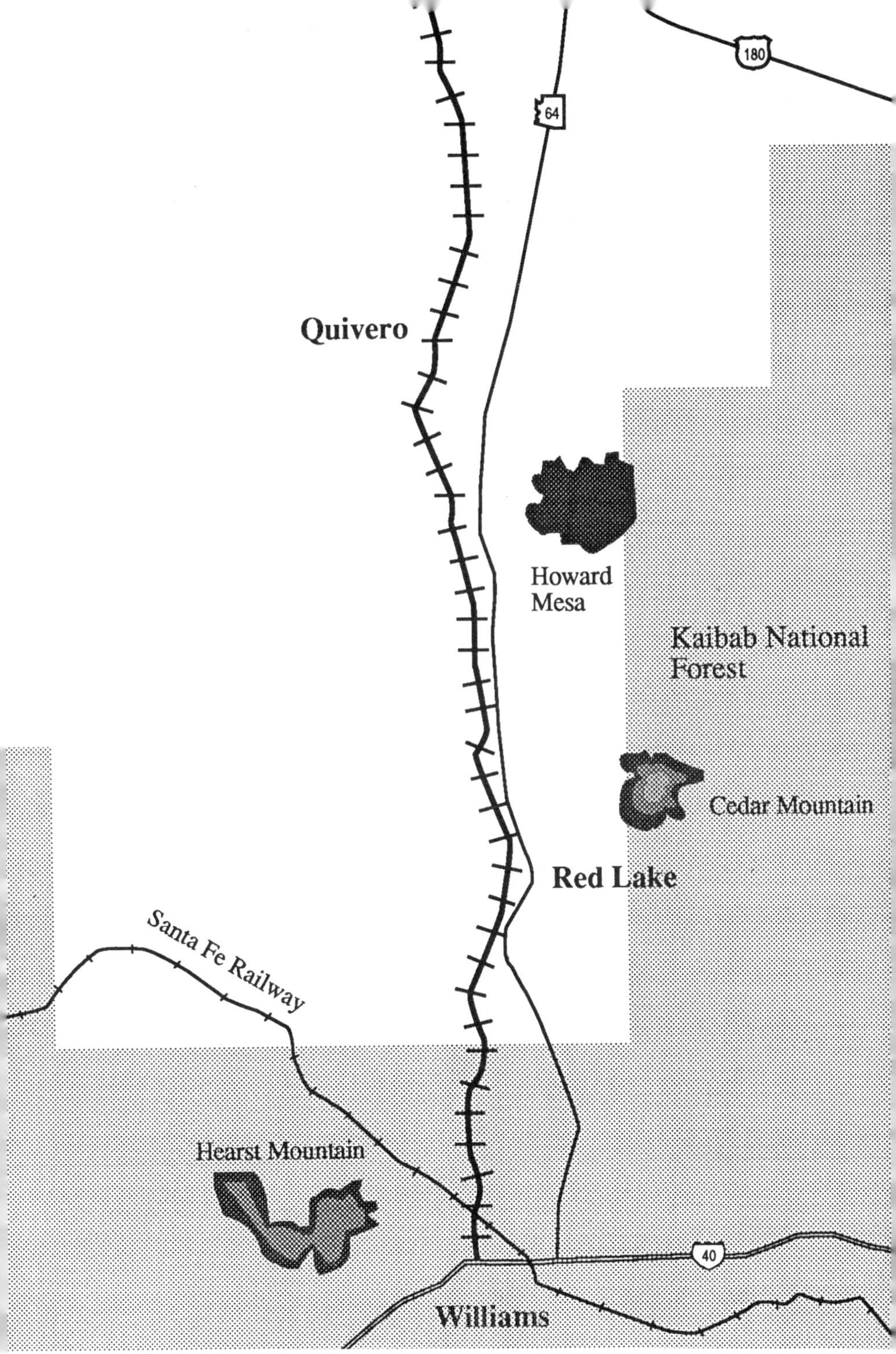

Route of the Grand Canyon Railway

Milepost 34: Red Butte Mountain, elevation 7,370 feet, a brilliant sandstone peak, is the solitary mountain rising above the horizon several miles to the northeast. It is visible for many miles in all directions. Called by the Havasupai Indians "hue-ga-da-wi-za" or "Mountain of the Clenched Fist," this promontory was described by Lt. Beale on September 15, 1857:

"The most prominent landmark in view, ...of curious form, rising out of the plain and entirely isolated ... the sides quite red about halfway up and the shape of the whole somewhat resembles a bishop's mitre."

In the custom of the day, Beale named the peak for Lt. C. E. Thornburn, USN, who was in charge of the itinerary report for the expedition. The name has not stuck, perhaps because "Red Butte" is more descriptive. The mountain sports a basaltic cap dating from its volcanic eruptions in the Cenozoic era. This hard cap has saved it from the wind and water erosion which has levelled its former neighbors, making it stand alone in the barren expanse where once other mountains of lesser strength stood.

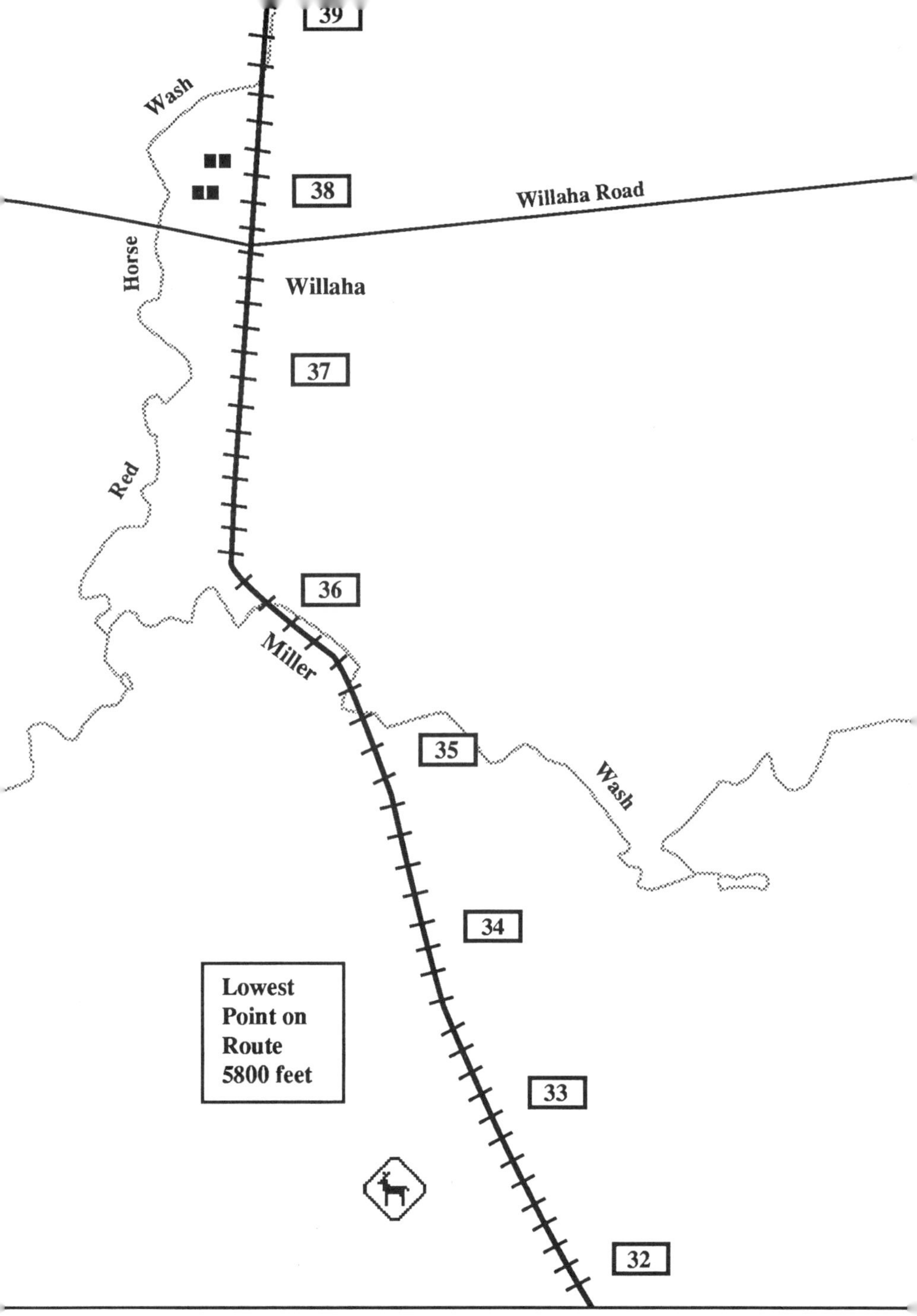

Milepost 32-39

Red Butte is an isolated pile of grey and red shales and red sandstone protected by a 125 foot cap of basalt. These types of rock layers formerly covered all the Kaibab limestone of this plateau to a thickness of at least 800 feet. The small remnant remaining in Red Butte has been protected by the hard basalt at the top.

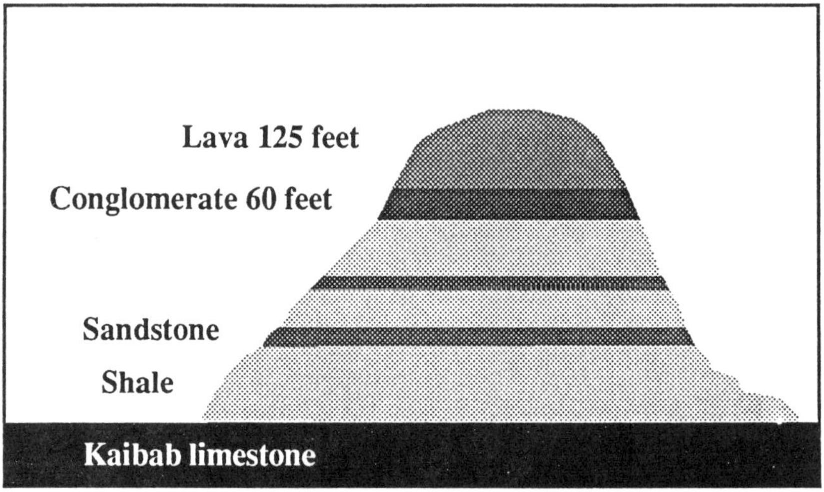

Section through Red Butte Mountain near milepost 45. Millions of years ago this valley was filled with similar peaks but without the basaltic cap which has prevented erosion.

The Butte appears to have been of great interest to the Native Americans living in its vicinity. The Havasupais have a tradition that many years ago a large spring of water flowed from near its base, but in the great convulsion of nature which changed the current of the waters of Havasupai Creek, the spring disappeared and never has been seen since. Though it is hard to know how to interpret this legend, there are some factual counterparts. Stands of quaking aspen on the butte show that water is still in the area. Furthermore, Red Horse Wash flows from east to west along the south side of the butte and, in a major storm, can reach violent proportions, even to the point of wrecking a train, as it did in the summer of 1916.

Early maps of Red Butte suggest that mining claims were located at its base and that silver mining was carried on here as early as 1650.

The original Grand Canyon Airport opened in 1928 at the small airstrip on the north side of Red Butte, an area 18 miles south of the Canyon where the old Maine-Grand Canyon stage route touches the mountain.

<u>Milepost 36</u>: Miller Wash cuts deeply back and forth under the tracks here, flowing northwest toward the Canyon. Its name probably comes from P. C. Miller, who built a cabin nearby and ran cattle here at the turn of the century. The black bed of an old passing track extends a mile on the east, parallel to the mainline.

<u>Mileposts 36-37</u>: Northbound trains begin a slow ascent; southbound trains continue to descend to the bottom of the ancient sea which once covered this area. Cross-country transmission wires cross above the tracks.

<u>Milepost 38</u>: Willaha, elevation 5,900 feet, is the name given this vanished settlement. The name is probably a Supai Indian word for "watering place." It has been suggested that it may possibly be a corruption of "Valhalla," the palatial afterlife in Scandinavian mythology which influenced the Swedish lumberjacks living north of here in Apex at milepost 52. There is a "Walhalla" (Valhalla) Plateau in the Canyon which received its name from Francois Matthes, a German-educated cartographer who named many of the Canyon formations for Norse gods and Scandinavian myths.

In any event, there is nothing palatial here and very little to suggest a "watering place." The area is very arid in the early summer. The railroad formerly hauled water to the stockmen living near here. Loading pens for cattle are still visible, along with the bed of a 24-car siding used for loading cattle, sheep and water cars. An old water tank, warehouse, box car shed, and ancient bunk house built by the Santa Fe in 1919 for the DeRyder Ranch are the sentinel structures east of the tracks south of milepost 38. The concrete ruins of the original station rest on the east side of the tracks just north of Willaha Road.

At this point, Willaha Road crosses the tracks and continues westward to the Havasupai Indian reservation, the only permanent settlement in the bottom of the Canyon. Supai is its official name.

Despite the aridity of the immediate area, Cataract Canyon is subject to severe flooding during August monsoons. In 1911 a rim-to-rim, forty-foot wall of water swept away all buildings in Supai while the Indians clung helplessly to the cliff walls.

Before the railroad was built, Cataract Canyon west of the tracks served as the route for the Bass Stagecoach from Ash Fork and Williams to the Canyon. Billy Bass thought the Cataract route smoother and safer than the competing routes from Maine (now the town of Parks) and Flagstaff. This route later allowed him to meet northbound trains here during construction of the railroad.

Milepost 39: Red Horse Wash, elevation 6,000 feet, crosses under the tracks, flowing toward the west when it is running. Water comes from the run-off from Red Butte farther east, which now almost drops from view. Ordinarily

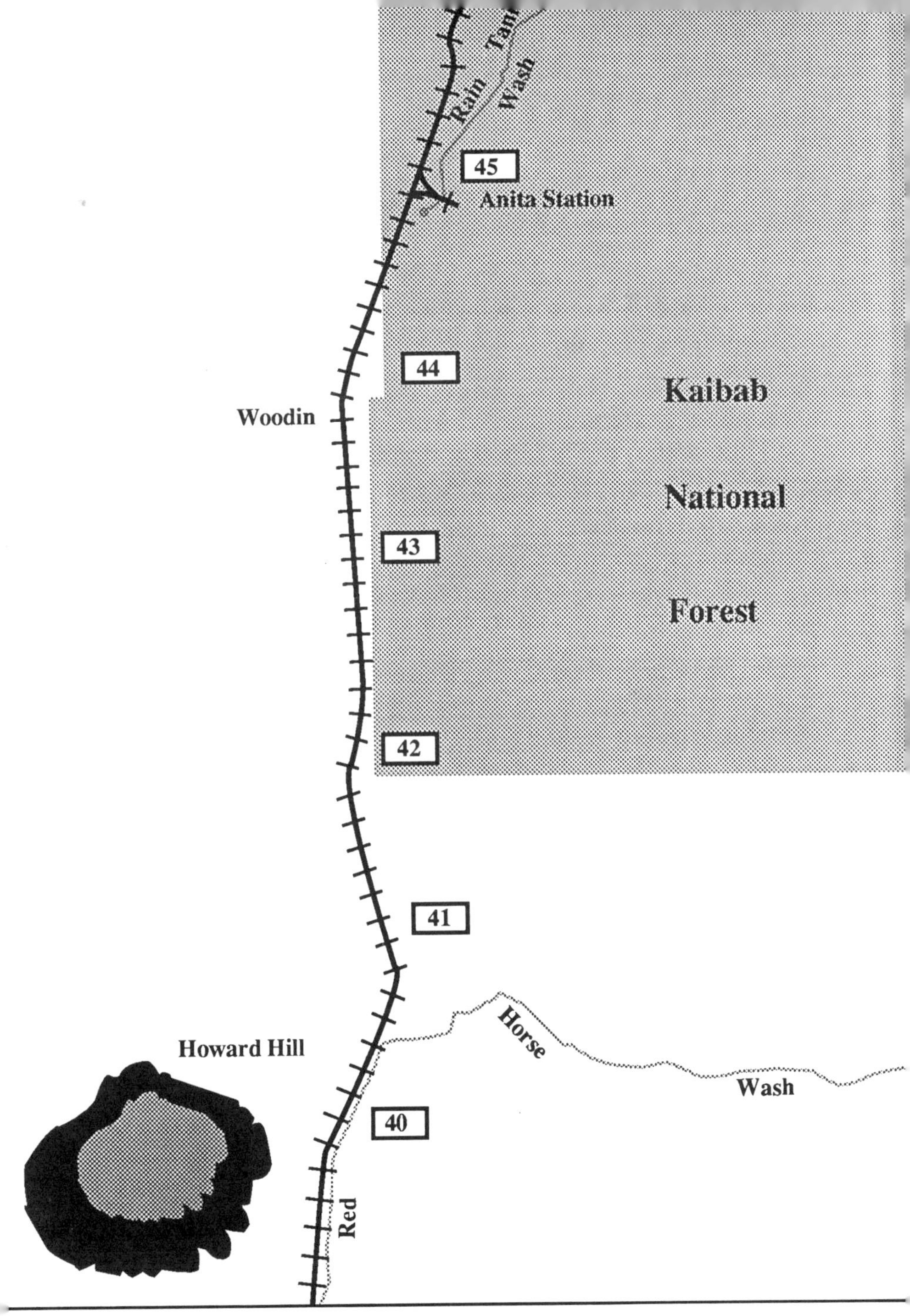

Milepost 40-45

dry, this wash becomes a wall of water in intense storms. On July 29, 1916, it washed out the bridge and wrecked the night train from the Canyon, killing its fireman. Trains now slow to 30 m.p.h. here.

Friar Francisco Garces camped here in July 1776, en route to the Canyon. He named this wash "Pozo de Santa Isabel." He continued on from this point to become the first white man to meet the Cerbat Tribe at the bottom of the Canyon. It was on this same journey that he gave the Colorado River its lasting name.

Mile 40.5: Several miles east are the Red Horse and Moqui Stage Station ruins, which served as resting places for Canyon stages from Maine and Flagstaff between 1892 and 1901.

Milepost 42: North of here limestone mesas are visible which ages ago were the banks of an ancient sea. Fossils of sea animals have been found imbedded in the limestone. These mesas contain the copper ore which motivated building the railroad.

Mile 43.8: Woodin, elevation 5,930 feet, possibly a corrupted English spelling of Wodin (Odin), the chief divinity in Scandinavian mythology, is the name given this former station. Though its origins are unclear, the name may have been given to the area by Swedish immigrant lumberjacks living at the Saginaw and Manistee Lumber Company farther north at Apex. In the early days of the railroad a one-car spur existed here to spot water cars and to load cattle and sheep for the Pittman Valley Land and Cattle Company.

At Woodin northbound trains parallel the Kaibab National Forest boundary lying immediately to the east.

Southbound trains leave the Kaibab Forest at this point and descend into the bed of the ancient sea described at mileposts 30-31.

Milepost 45: Anita, elevation 5,920 feet, a former mining settlement, now a ghost town, is the name given this turn-of-the century, once flourishing area at the junction of the tracks and Rain Tank Wash. The surrounding limestone mesas and cliffs, once the northern shores of the saltwater sea, contain scattered, deep ore deposits which prompted the building of the railroad. A small station, section house and cistern were located here on the west from the early days of the railroad. The remnants of each are visible opposite milepost 45 immediately north of Anita Road. In 1899, Bass stagecoaches met trains here to transport passengers the remaining 20 miles to the Canyon.

Intermittent passenger service to Anita began on March 15, 1900. The Santa Fe and Grand Canyon RR issued time cards showing the schedule to Anita, where passengers changed to a Bass stage for the remaining 20 miles:

Santa Fe & Grand Canyon R. R.

TIME CARD.

No. 10.	Miles	March 15, 1900.	No. 11.
P. M.			P. M.
12:30	0	Lv.....WILLIAMS.....Ar	6:30
1:00	9	.......RED LAKE.......	6:00
1:35	20	..........PRADO..........	5:30
2:00	29	..........VALLE..........	5:00
2:30	38	........WILLAHA........	4:30
3:00	45	...ANITA JUNCTION...	4:00
3:15	47	..........ANITA..........	3:45
		STAGE	
4:30	55	.........COCONINO.........	2:30
6:00	67	Ar..GRAND CANYON.Lv	1:30
P. M.			P. M.

First timetable issued by the "Santa Fe & Grand Canyon RR" Company in March 1900. The timetable is incorrect in its mileage both to Anita and to the Canyon.

Anita acquired its name from the daughter of Tom Lombard, one of the principal investors in the railroad and one of several mine owners in the area. Rich but scattered ore deposits in the surrounding mesas to the north–many still there–prompted feverish mining by 31 companies from 1880 to 1910. The mines extended over a range of six miles, mostly in Rain Tank Wash Canyon northeast of the tracks. Their names spoke of great expectations: Copper Prince, Copper Queen, Copper King, Anita Queen, After Thought, Commodore Dewey, Eastern Star, and Grandview. Each was extensively mined, the deepest pits reaching 530 feet.

Twenty families lived here until 1940. An ore smelter sat where a side track left the mainline at milepost 45 to run 2.87 miles east to the mines at Anita Camp. An ore loading ramp built by the Santa Fe in 1918 is still visible east of the tracks just south of Anita Road. A 40-car wye existed here during mining days along with a 12-car track for water cars. The south leg of the original wye can be seen just south of Anita Road; the north leg's roadbed is visible where it originally joined the mainline at milepost 45.

To the east is Rain Tank Wash Canyon. On its southern edges lie the original Anita mines. The roadbed of the original spur line is visible off to the east as it curves and ascends into the piñons along the limestone cliffs. The original ties are still in place along the roadbed, and some of the metal remains.

Some trackside wooden structures still sit, collapsed, alongside the roadbed. Foundations, both stone and wood, of miners' homes dot the landscape, which is cluttered with rusting tin cans, bottles, shovels, ore cans and buckets. Entrances to the original mines dot the area. The original roadbed of the spur is graded in a gradual ascent from west to east, so that loaded cars of ore could be sent down the rails to Anita Junction, 2.87 miles away, simply by the force of gravity.

After leaving Anita, northbound trains re-enter the Kaibab National Forest, which now lies on both sides of the tracks. Northbound trains begin a long uphill climb at 25 m.p.h to Apex. Southbound trains from Anita enter a long level grade for some 30 miles.

Mileposts 46-47: The train parallels deep canyons to the east carved by Rain Tank Wash. As the elevation increases, piñon and juniper reappear in greater numbers along the limestone cliffs.

Mature Piñon Pine

Milepost 48: Piñon pine begin to reappear, often in company with juniper. Piñon pines (pinus edulis) flourish at lower elevations between roughly 3,500 and 5,000 feet. They can be seen south of Quivero and north of Anita en route to the Canyon. The piñon is the most common pine of the Upper Sonoran Life zone. It extends from the Sonoran plains of Mexico northward into Colorado and Utah. It has a Christmas tree shape when it is small and, unlike ponderosas, has small unbunched needles. Many piñons grow adjacent to the tracks and in valleys between mileposts 50-60. Piñon nuts ripen in the fall and are ready for collection by November. Indians inhabiting these areas collect piñon nuts as an important part of their diet.

Mature Alligator Juniper

Alligator Juniper (juniperus deppeana), so named for its rough bark, is another popular tree which shares soil and elevation with piñon. It is commonly miscalled "cedar" due to its aroma. Along with piñon it comprises the scrub or pygmy forests of the Kaibab. It is extensively used for fence posts and firewood. Indians have many uses for its berries in the preparation of medicine. Extracts of berries and twigs are used in cleansing ceremonies and purification rites.

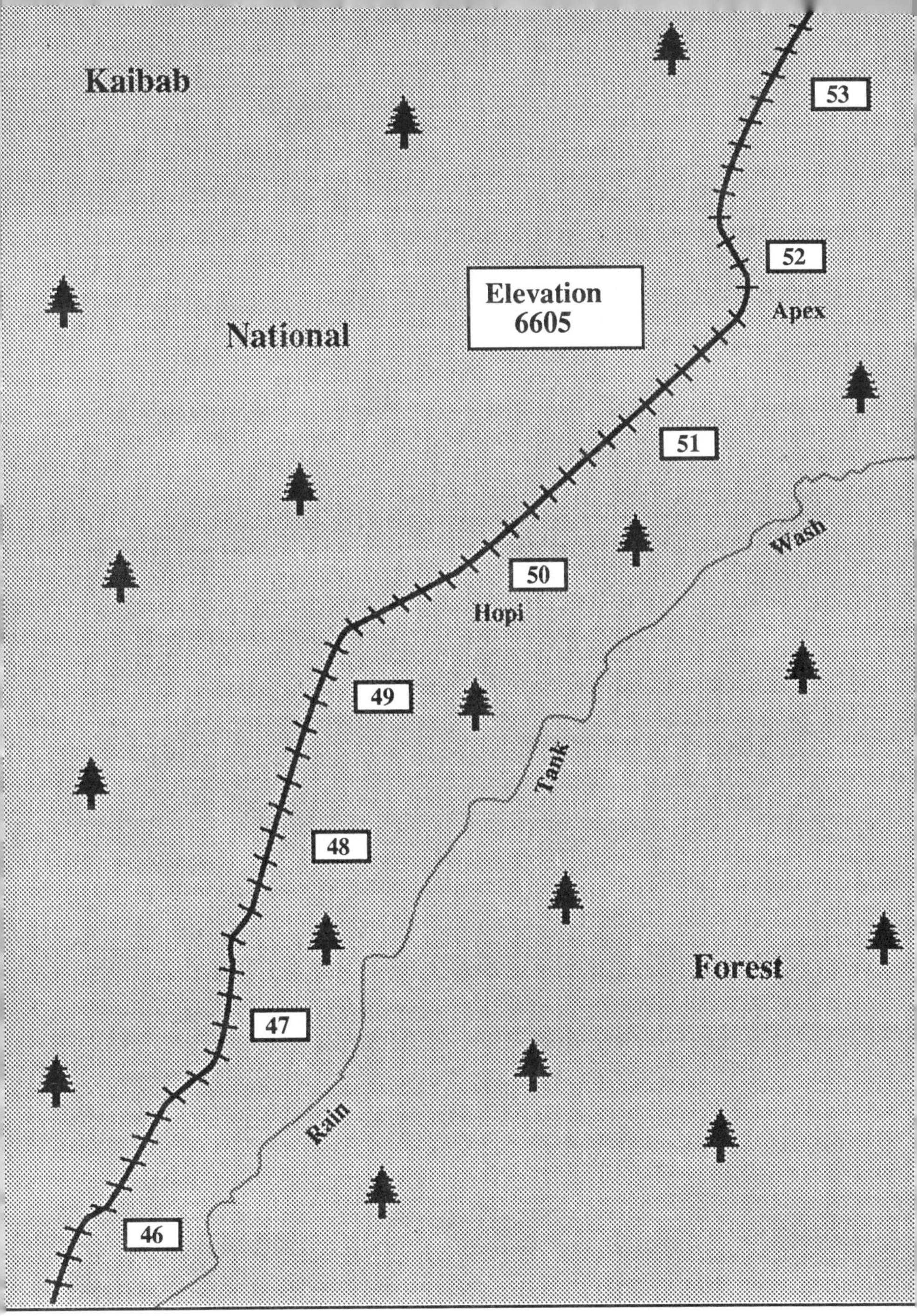

Milepost 46-53

Some juniper trees live to almost biblical ages. In the Kaibab Forest near Williams and along the Canyon some juniper have trunks more than five feet in diameter, indicating that they were growing well before the Pilgrims landed at Plymouth Rock in 1620.

Milepost 50: Hopi is the name for this one-time station whose name derives from the Anasazi Indians living here about A.D. 1200. The Anasazi were ancestors of modern Hopi. A passing track once was here along with a 23-car siding. From Hopi northward ledges of Kaibab limestone appear. These ledges are tilted slightly southward, so that they rise as one approaches the Canyon.

Hopi Indians at one time lived not only here but farther east along the Canyon rim, notably at the Tusayan Ruin on the rim east of Grand Canyon Village. The Hopi are one of several Indian nations still populating the area.

The rectangle formed by the Canyon's south rim, Williams and Flagstaff contains a wide variety of Indian cultures. Havasupai Indians, the descendants of the Cerbat, still live as they have for centuries in the bottom of the Grand Canyon in beautiful Cataract Canyon, formed by Cataract Creek which crosses under the railroad at milepost 4. "Havasupai" means "people of the blue-green water," a name for their majestic waterfalls. The blue-green color derives from lime eroding into the water from limestone rocks nearby.

The Tusayan Pueblo east of Grand Canyon Village attests to Anasazi, ancestors of the modern Hopi, living on the Canyon's rim in the 12th and 13th centuries.

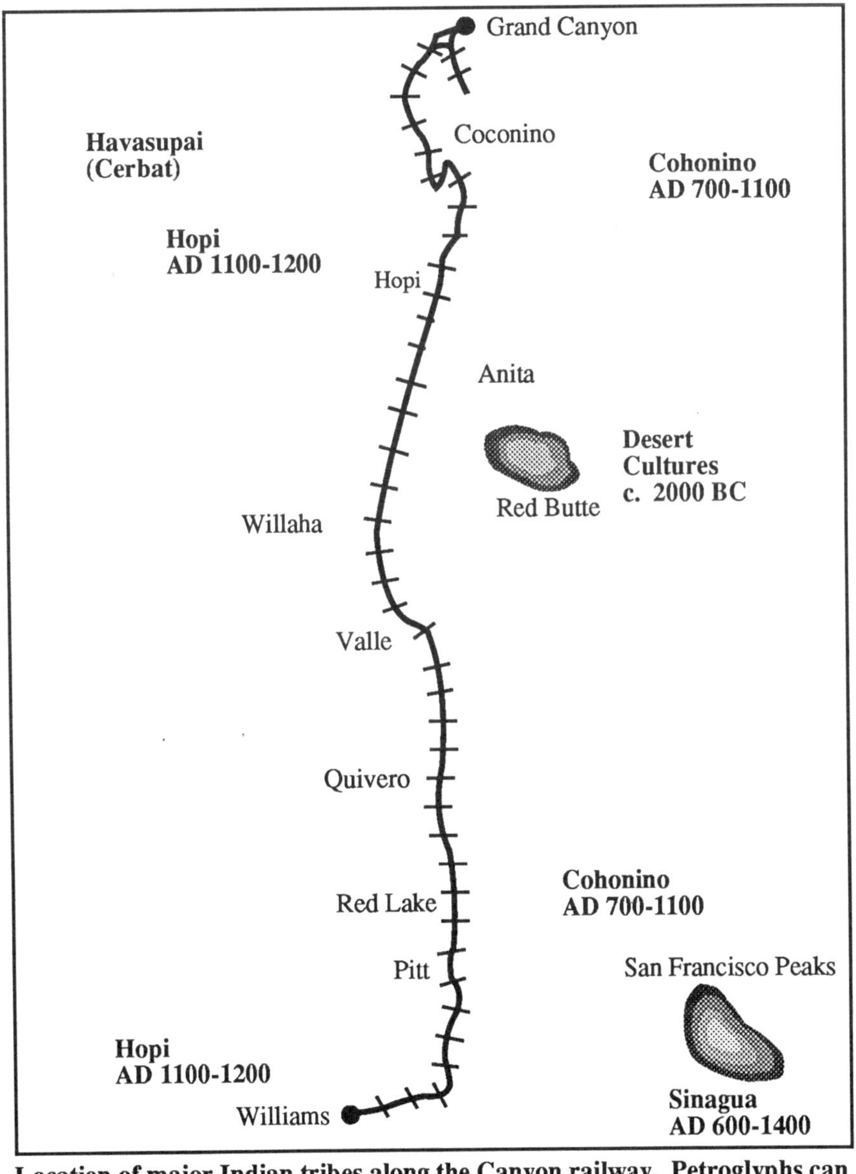

Location of major Indian tribes along the Canyon railway. Petroglyphs can still be found on rock formations near the tracks.

Remnants of the Desert Cultures, an ancient tribe predating most of the other tribes in this area, have been found atop massive Red Butte Mountain immediately south of the Canyon and adjacent to the railroad near milepost 41. The Navajo tribe occupies a vast reservation at the east end of the Canyon extending south almost to Flagstaff. The Indians called Sinagua ("without water") flourished from about A.D. 600 to 1400 north, south, and east of the San Francisco Peaks. Closest to the railroad tracks are the remnants of the Cohonino Indians who lived at various spots along the Williams-Canyon corridor between A.D. 700-1100.

All of these tribes, many of whose descendants are still present, contribute to the Native American culture of the area. More than a thousand differing artifacts of Indian cultures have been found in the Canyon. Common to all these tribes is a respect for high places as being especially sacred because of access to Indian gods. This is particularly true of Humphrey's Peak in the San Francisco cluster, Bill Williams Mountain near Williams and Red Butte just south of the Canyon. Worship sites still sit atop some of these peaks.

From a purely historical viewpoint, these cultures have contributed names to areas along the railroad. "Moqui" for the Moqui Lodge near milepost 61 is a Hopi word for "vanishing." "Willaha" at milepost 38 is a Havasupai name for "watering place." "Hopi" at milepost 50 attests to Hopis once living there, just as "Coconino Wash" in the canyon of that name near milepost 57 recalls Cohonino Indians who lived in that canyon.

Despite individual tribal differences, Indian cultures in this area still speak to the world with respect for ancestors, for signs and symbols, and for the environment. Travelers in these lands should respect the ancient traditions of their heritage as they pass through.

Milepost 52: Apex, elevation 6,605 feet, is the name for this one-time lumbering settlement which has vanished. It acquired its name because it was thought to be the highest point on the railroad between Williams and the Canyon. In fact, the Canyon's south rim is higher, but Apex acquired that distinction from being the top of the long uphill climb beginning at Anita eight miles south.

Apex was once the site of a station located west of the tracks and housing for a section crew. There was a 31-car siding here. The remains of the white concrete bunkhouse still loom dramatically amid ponderosa pines and piñons just north of milepost 52.

Ponderosa pines are the dominant trees on both sides of the tracks. In 1928 the Saginaw and Manistee Lumber Company, headquartered in Williams, located a field headquarters one mile east of the mainline and commenced large-scale lumbering operations. It built an 85-car wye and spur, a double track, and a 27-car siding. Eventually there were 26 miles of temporary track running into the forest. The families living here were Swedish immigrants whose breadwinners were involved in cutting and loading felled ponderosa pines onto flat cars. The pines were used, in part, for railroad ties and for building tourist facilities at the Canyon. The little community lived for the most part in converted boxcars, although supervisors lived in more traditional homes, some of which were moved to Williams in the early 1940s. In 1929 a one-room schoolhouse opened here in a converted boxcar.

After 1935 lumbering operations ceased. The railroad removed most of the relics of this hamlet, although a few foundations, smaller structures, pots, pans and cans can still be found near the bed of the old wye.

The bed of the original wye is clearly visible on the east directly opposite milepost 52. The railroad plans a connecting track here via the wye bed through the old lumbering area to connect with the terminal at Grand Canyon Airport four miles east, to transport air passengers directly to the Canyon by rail.

After passing Apex, northbound trains slow to 20 m.p.h. Forest road 335 parallels and then crosses the tracks north of Apex.

Milepost 53: Tusayan, elevation 6,000 feet, is the name given the considerable village lying several miles east of the track along highway 64. Its name comes from the Hopi name "Tusqua" given to their ancestral lands. The Anasazi Indians ("the ancient ones") lived in this area between A.D. 700 and 1200. The Tusayan Ruin, located on the east rim at the Canyon, has a small museum detailing the history of the area. The Tusayan Pueblo, excavated in the 1930s, probably housed 20 persons. About A.D. 1200 the Anasazi left Tusayan and the Canyon area and moved to lower elevations to the east. Hopi Indians are their modern descendants. The Cardenas portion of the Coronado Expedition visited the Canyon near Tusayan in 1540 with Hopi guides.

Modern Tusayan is a flourishing tourist-oriented town serving Canyon visitors. It lies two miles south of the Canyon entrance station and is surrounded by the Kaibab Forest.

Milepost 54: The most prevalent tree of the Kaibab Forest and most likely to be seen in the dense forests at the northern and southern ends of the route to the Canyon is the ponderosa (pinus ponderosa). When mature it is sometimes called the "western yellow pine" because of the orangish-yellow cast to its bark. Young ponderosa lack this characteristic color and for that reason are sometimes called "black jack." Ponderosa grow densely in the Kaibab, particularly at elevations between 6,000-8,000 feet. In areas where there is sufficient clay, ponderosa grow tall, stately, and symmetrical, sometimes to 100 feet in height, with trunks too thick to embrace. Two hundred years of age is not uncommon. Ponderosas grow where the annual precipitation is 18-24 inches, less water than any other large commercial tree requires. At lower elevations it is found with junipers, piñons, and oaks. In its main range, pure stands are the norm. On cool northern slopes and at upper elevations it mixes with Douglas Fir, spruce, limber pine and white fir. Small aspen groves also mingle with ponderosa at higher elevations.

Mature Ponderosa Pine

Milepost 55: Coconino Wash and canyon, elevation 6,411 feet. The roadbed here curves through the narrow canyon carved by Coconino Wash. When the rails were first laid, this area was difficult to construct. The wash lies immediately east of the roadbed and a limestone wall hugs the west side of the track. There are two horseshoe curves almost back-to-back where Coconino Wash twice cuts under the tracks. Both ends of the train can be seen at the same time. The serpentine curves and steep 3.22% grade here prompted the Santa Fe to build a simulated section of this portion of the route as a training exercise for its engineers.

Construction of this section of track was made difficult by the wash and the narrow canyon walls. By June 1900 the rails extended to milepost 53. By October, it had progressed only three miles. Construction froze here for almost a year, due not only to the frigid weather and difficult construction but also because of the insolvency of the original line. During that period sporadic passenger service carried passengers to this area, where they changed from the train to one of Billy Bass's stagecoaches for the remaining leg of the trip. The original Bass Trail is still visible as a dusty road crossing and recrossing the rails.

Milepost 56: Animal life here includes both the turkey and the mountain lion, plus an occasional bear. Wild turkeys are native to this area. By late fall, gobblers weigh 18 pounds and hens as much as 10 pounds. They breed in late Spring. The female lays 9-12 eggs in a shallow depression in the ground near an old log or pile of brush close to drinking water. The young hatch simultaneously about a month after the eggs are laid. They instinctively follow the mother, who frequently joins with other hens and offspring to form large flocks.

Young turkeys eat insects. As they grow older, they approach an adult diet of acorns, pine seeds, grass, berries and green leaves. Although they are seldom seen from highways, they can frequently be seen along back roads, especially near a clump of oak, which is common in this area. The wary birds will usually run if startled.

The sight of a roaming mountain lion is a thrilling experience. They appear as a large house cat. Most of them have fur which is tan or gray, with a white underbelly. Mature lions weigh from 80 to 200 pounds. Young lions are born in

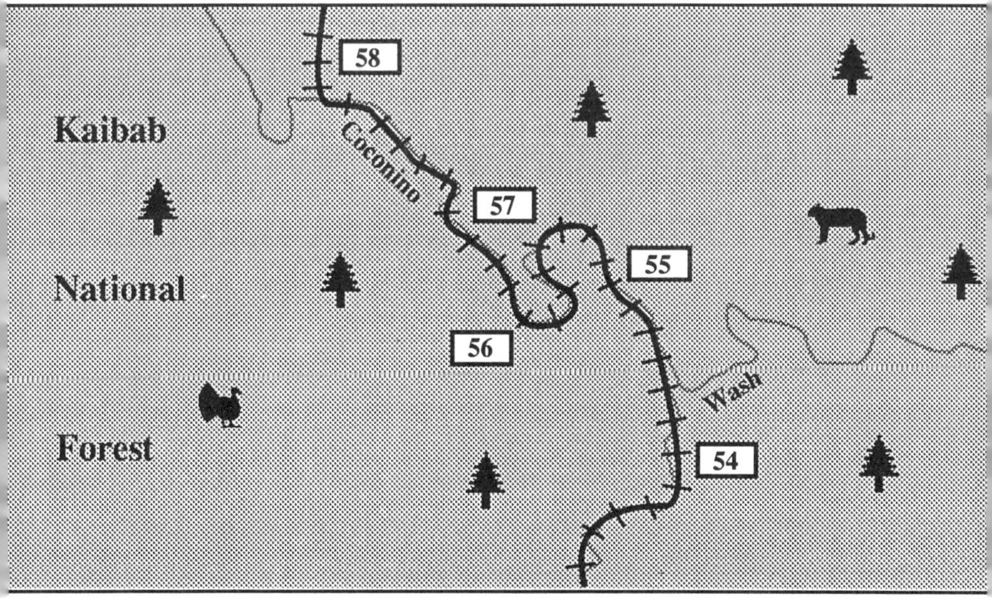

Milepost 54-58

litters of two to three in the spring after a three-month gestation. The young stay with the mother for a period of several months until they feed on their own. Lions are true predators. They feed on weak, old and diseased deer, elk, porcupines and sometimes domestic livestock. They are strongly territorial.

Gambel's Oak

Bears are shy animals who usually live in areas with thick cover. The color of the only bear now living in Arizona, the black bear, ranges from true black to reddish brown. Adults weigh from 125 to 450 pounds. They are omnivorous, eating grass, nuts, berries, insects, honey and flesh of other animals.

Bears are Arizona's largest remaining predator. They breed in the summer. The young are usually twins born during winter hibernation. They remain with their mothers for one or two years.

These animals are unusually shy and prefer to run away rather than provoke a confrontation. If you are lucky enough to see one from the train, the best places are likely to be in thick underbrush where there are acorns or berries.

Milepost 57: Northbound trains enter a long uphill grade. Limestone rock ledges decorate the east side of the canyon. Coconino Indians lived in these ledges and similar rock formations between A.D. 700-1050, coexisting for a time with the Anasazi. Limestone rocks and the presence of water in Coconino Wash, coupled with extensive tree and undergrowth cover, have also encouraged animals to live in the area, notably turkeys, mountain lions, and occasional bears. There can be deep snow in winter. To the east of the tracks is a mature ponderosa pine whose curved trunk probably was bent into a sideways "U" shape by heavy snows pinning it down in its youth.

Shortly north of milepost sign 57 sit the station and section house ruins at "Coconino," elevation 6,411 feet. The concrete remains of the original station are visible on the east side of the tracks. Loading pens and a 34-car passing track and siding east of the tracks once served cattle, sheep and logging operations here. The bed of the original passing track lies in dark cinders immediately east of the main track. There was once a section house for four men with an outside cistern, the remains of which can be seen west of the tracks. Just north of the original concrete station is a wood and pile bridge which crosses over the original Bass trail.

Midway between mileposts 57 and 58 the track makes an eastward turn at "Tooker Cut". Limestone ledges press close to both sides of the rails.

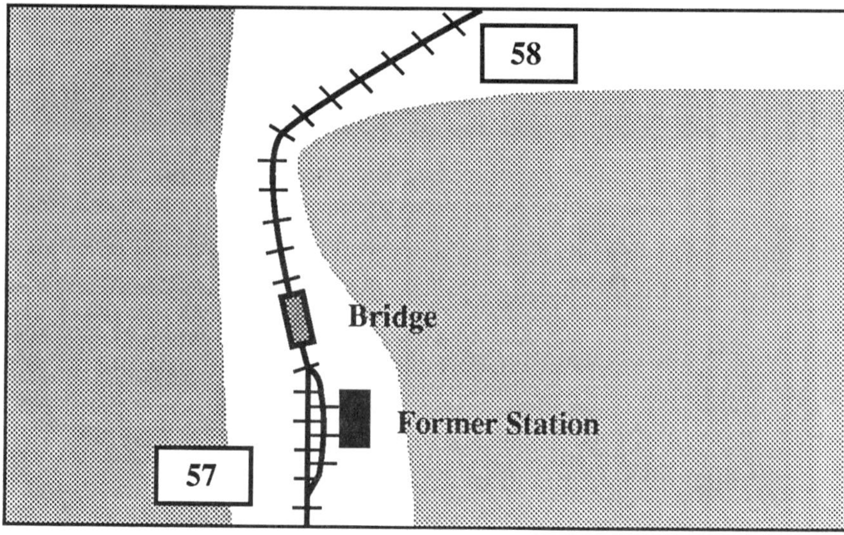

Coconino Canyon, with narrow Tooker Cut near milepost 58, site of a serious wreck in 1939.

A dramatic wreck occurred here at nighttime on July 27, 1939, when the first of three southbound trains took the curve too fast, left the track and partially derailed against the west limestone cut. The boiler on the wrecked engine burst, sending steam into the moonlit sky. Engineers on the two following trains realized the unusual steam escape as abnormal and came to a stop before entering Tooker curve. Fifty-one persons were injured but there were no fatalities.

Milepost 58: A private cabin sits near an old mine on the east side of the tracks.

Mile 58.5: Forest Road 328 crosses the tracks here. It leads east to Moqui Lodge, a historic lodge at the entrance to Grand Canyon Park. The word "Moqui" is a Hopi Indian word for "vanishing," which refers to a small group of Hopi Indians who left their tribe to the east and settled here. They were called "Moqui" because they had vanished from the tribe.

The original Bass Trail again meets the tracks, crossing and re-crossing several times. At present the trail serves as access to picnic areas and to the Canyon's sanitation services and water reclamation plant.

Milepost 59: North of milepost 59 the ascent becomes steeper. Trains slow to 10 m.p.h.

Milepost 60: Dense ponderosa forests. Early tourists were much taken by the majesty of these surroundings. In 1915, a U.S. Geological Survey geologist surveying the area wrote:

"Here it seems as if one were suddenly transported to England, and were passing through a succession of landed estates, without, however, finding the accompanying mansions. Aisles of stately trees, nature planted and grown, yet as perfectly in line as if set with mathematical precision, lead the eye into open glades where deer and antelope move to an fro, and where one looks instinctively for the bold facade of an historic building or the battlemented towers of some romantic castle."

The history of the site is, alas, more prosaic. From 1899 to early 1901 the track ended here. Passengers changed to Billy Bass's stagecoaches for the final leg to the rim. The track was finally completed to the rim in September 1901. The southern boundary of Grand Canyon National Park is near milepost 60.

Milepost 61: Rowe's Well, or Rowe Well, elevation 6,681 feet, is the name for the well and former hotel located in this pine and piñon thicket by Sanford Rowe, a pioneer stockman and stagecoach guide who in June 1890 was told by John Hance that water could be found here. Rowe inspected the area and found deer tracks with dirt standing between the hoof marks, indicating moisture near the surface. He began digging and hit solid rock at 18 feet. He placed a monument of rocks atop the hole since he had already used his homestead right. He then developed the well and a small two-story hotel for stagecoach visitors. Later he used the area as an auto camp. Between 1910-1919 the chief ranger of the Grand Canyon Forest Reserve had his residence here. Today Rowe's Well is a picnic spot with a ramada adjacent to the tracks in a clearing on the west just south of milepost 61.

Milepost 62: The train continues through dense ponderosa pines. Maswik Lodge and its cabins lie on the east under the trees.

Milepost 63: "Lombard," elevation 6,850 feet. Northbound trains emerge from a long uphill curve which points them eastward parallel to the rim of the Canyon, which is now on the left or north side of the tracks. As trains emerge from this curve, three structures appear—Red Horse Stage Station, Buckey O'Neill's cabin, and Bright Angel Lodge.

The westernmost of the cabins adjoining Bright Angel Lodge is Red Horse Station, a stage stop originally located near Red Horse Wash on the Flagstaff and Maine stagecoach routes to the canyon. Ralph Cameron moved it to the rim, built a second story and used it for a while as a small hotel. From 1910 to 1935 this building housed the U.S. Post Office for the Canyon. It is now used as a rental cabin for visitors.

East of Red Horse Station and immediately left of Bright Angel Lodge is Buckey O'Neill's original cabin. Like Red Horse Station, it too has been made a part of the cabin

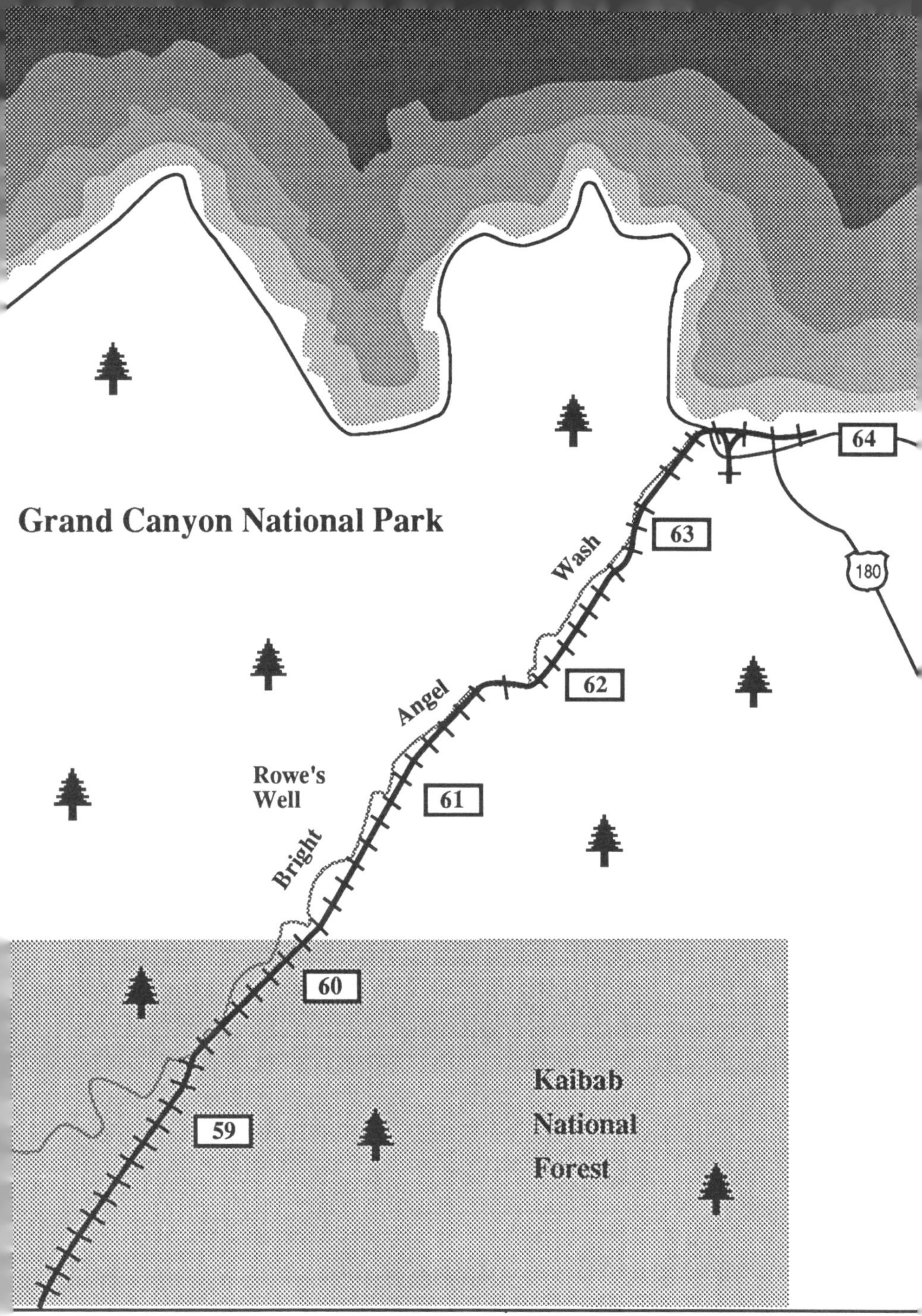

Milepost 59-64

complex at the lodge. Buckey O'Neill rightfully deserves the title of founder of the Canyon railroad. In his varied career he had been, at times, a prospector, promotor, Mayor of Prescott, and later one of Teddy Roosevelt's Rough Riders. He had a series of exciting western-style adventures at Tombstone and Prescott before becoming "respectable". He had earned the name "Buckey" for his skill in "bucking the tiger" at the faro table.

Buckey had read the inspiring account of the Canyon by William Randolph Hearst, the New York publisher who had written glowingly of his visit to the Canyon. Buckey visited the Canyon's south rim and liked it so much he immediately built a log cabin on the rim 20 feet from the edge. His original building still stands as part of the Bright Angel cabin complex. It is the first building on the left after leaving the Canyon side of the Bright Angel Lodge.

William "Bucky" O'Neill

Buckey truly loved the Canyon. He also loved its economic potential for silver, copper and asbestos mining. He used his cabin to do some preliminary research and soon filed a claim deep inside the Canyon at a place now known as O'Neill Butte. He also bought copper interests on the Coconino Plateau 20 miles south of the Canyon. While Buckey liked the Canyon and his mines a great deal, he disliked traveling there by stage. Beginning in 1893 he began to try to convince Thomas R. Lombard of the Chicago investment firm of Lombard, Goode and Company to fund a railroad from Williams to the site of his cabin on the rim via, of course, his ore claims 20 miles south.

Buckey preached the mining and railway gospel wherever he went. In 1897, thanks to Buckey's efforts, Lombard and Goode took a harrowing stage trip with Buckey to the Canyon. They saw the Canyon, Buckey's cabin, and-most importantly-the ore deposits. They quickly became convinced of the practicality of the line. Lombard agreed with Buckey's plan, got a map and modestly decided that the railroad's northern terminus at the rim would be named "Lombard" to commemorate his magnanimity and that the mining area 20 miles south of the rim should be named "Anita" after his daughter.

Rails were laid first on October 30, 1899. Buckey did not live to see the great day. After visiting his cabin for a last time and sailing to Cuba to fight in the Spanish-American War, he lost his life on July 1, 1898, killed by sniper fire the day before the charge up San Juan Hill by Roosevelt's Rough Riders. His cabin is a living reminder of the central role he played in bringing the railroad to the Canyon's rim. The Grand Canyon Railway has named the "Buckey O'Neill

Express" in his honor. His role has a more indelible mark on history than does that of Thomas Lombard, whose self-imposed name for this area has not lasted.

Bright Angel Lodge was a more contentious story. An original "Bright Angel Hotel" had been built in the late 1890s by John Hance. When the railroad arrived at the rim, it acquired this site and its buildings. Hostility developed at the small community at Grandview some 13 miles east where Hance and others had tourist-oriented facilities. Once the railroad arrived, the stage coaches to the rim soon ceased operating. The leading hotel prior to El Tovar, the Grandview, was put out of business, which did not endear the railroad to the Grandview community.

There were more problems. Peter Berry and Ralph Cameron were partners in a mining and hotel business at Grandview. Along with Cameron's brother Niles they had built the original Bright Angel Trail in 1891 to get to copper mines deep in the Canyon. Cameron charged a dollar toll to any miner or tourist who used the Bright Angel Trail. The Santa Fe objected; it hoped to build a new hotel on the old site of the original Bright Angel Hotel and wanted no impediment to tourist use. A struggle began between Cameron and the Santa Fe. Cameron renamed the trail the "Cameron Trail." He claimed land inside the Canyon along the trail and at Indian Gardens which the Santa Fe was promoting as a tourist outing.

When the railroad first arrived at the rim in 1901, its original station was a boxcar structure near the original Bright Angel Hotel. Cameron promptly built a hotel close to this station to cash in on the tourist trade from the arriving passengers. The Santa Fe then moved its terminal to the present site some 300 yards farther east so that passengers leaving trains would first come to El Tovar and would have to backtrack to reach Cameron's hotel.

Cameron retaliated by placing mining claims on the land which the Santa Fe intended to use for the new Bright Angel Hotel. He sought to box in the Santa Fe by placing mining claims all along the rim and deep in the Canyon as far as Indian Gardens. Nineteen lawsuits sprouted against Cameron from many sides. In 1906 Coconino County took over the "Cameron Trail" but Cameron continued to operate it and retained most of the profits for himself. The federal government finally obtained the trail from the County and put Cameron out of the trail business.

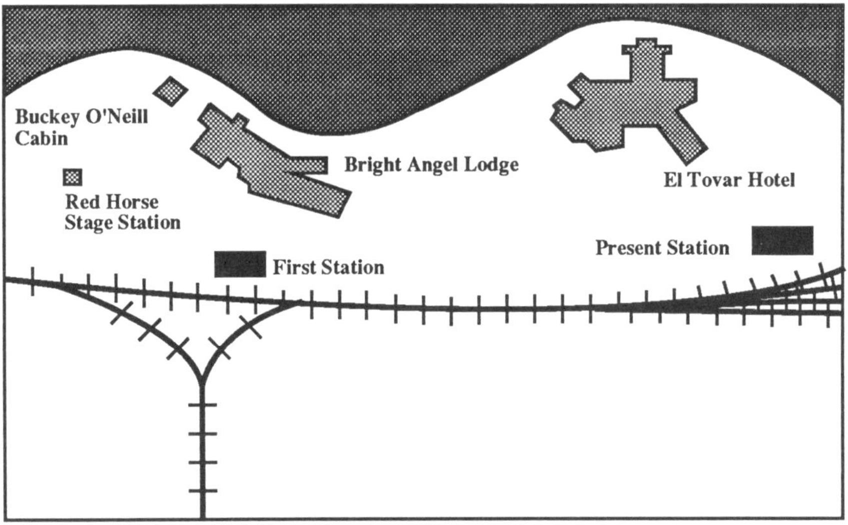

The original historic buildings at the Canyon terminus of the railroad. The original depot, labeled "first station," was intended to feed passengers to Bright Angel Hotel. It was demolished when El Tovar opened closer to the present depot.

For three decades Cameron used mining laws to tie up his lands along the rim and in the Canyon so that no one else could access them. The Santa Fe built the Hermit Trail farther west to give access to the Colorado River, and in 1919 the National Park Service completed the toll-free Kaibab Trail which undercut Cameron's business. Cameron's election to the House of Representatives and later to the U.S. Senate hastened his physical departure from the Canyon.

With Cameron out of the way, the Santa Fe's Canyon architect, Mary Jane Colter, designed the new Bright Angel Lodge in a pioneer style with natural wood tones like the original hotel on the site. After years of delays caused by the first World War and the depression, Bright Angel Lodge opened in 1935 along with a cluster of historic cabins, including Red Horse Stage Station and Buckey O'Neill's cabin, both saved through the good efforts of Mary Jane Colter.

Mile 63.5: The grade crossing at Bright Angel Lodge offers the only view into the Canyon from the railroad.

Milepost 64: Grand Canyon, elevation 6,875 feet. The yard limit is 1/4 mile prior to the depot. On the south lies the wye for turn-around, as well as the original powerhouse, mule barn, and present community building. The train station is the rustic log building on the north directly below El Tovar Hotel. This depot is the second in the area. An early board-and-batten depot was built in 1901 after the first train arrived. The Santa Fe moved the station farther to the east near El Tovar to attract train passengers to its hotel rather than allowing them to de-train at competitor hotels.

The present impressive station, the only log-cabin-style station on the Santa Fe line, dates from 1909. It is built of stained pines matching the majestic El Tovar Hotel. The depot was deeded by the Santa Fe to the National Park Service. It has become part of the Grand Canyon Historic District and has an honored place on the National Register of Historic Places. The National Park service has restored it faithfully to the way it looked the day it opened, without the brash crowds of hawkers with megaphones cajoling arriving passengers toward tour busses and lodgings.

Railroad depot at the Canyon

For many rail visitors one of the most exciting occasions was arrival at the Grand Canyon station. What had been expected to be a quiet inspirational scene was quite the opposite. Passengers were greeted by hawkers along the track shouting through megaphones to drum up business for tour companies. Baggage carts rattled along the platforms as luggage was transferred to El Tovar. Hissing and banging filled the air as steam engines were uncoupled and backed into the wye to be turned around for the return trip. The editors of the Saturday Evening Post, vocal in advocating Grand Canyon as a national park, criticized this disrespectful scene at the station, remarking that this "leather-lunged yawp for trade" and business right at the rim was an outrage to the Canyon's sacredness.

EL TOVAR

Occupying a site 7,000 feet above sea level, within steps of the rim and the railroad depot, El Tovar commands a panorama without parallel in the world. Fourteen miles toward the horizon is the north rim of the Canyon, easily seen from the front porch of El Tovar. Seven miles almost straight down is the roaring Colorado River appearing as a silvery thread.

First tentatively named "Bright Angel Tavern," El Tovar was built to match its spectacular surroundings. It is a long, low, rambling structure, built of native boulders and pine and Douglas fir. The Santa Fe hired architect Charles Whittlesey to blend the proportions of a Swiss mountain chalet with a Norwegian villa. Hopi Indians did the construction at a cost of $250,000.

When opened in 1905, El Tovar had 100 bedrooms and 21 bathrooms. It featured such rare luxuries of the day as hot and cold water, steam heat, electric lights and room telephones. Its crowning jewel was the 15th-century-styled dining room overlooking the Canyon. For all this luxury early tourists paid from $3.50 to $4.50 per day or up to $8 for a suite.

El Tovar soon became a mecca rivaling the Canyon. Presidents Taft and Teddy Roosevelt were frequent guests. So famous did El Tovar become that some thought the Canyon detracted from the hotel's majesty. Naturalist John Burroughs wrote of meeting a woman at the Canyon who complained to him that the Canyon "was built too near the hotel."

El Tovar is named for Don Pedro Tovar, the Spanish conquistador linked with the discovery of the Canyon by Coronado's expedition in 1540.

The Santa Fe apparently liked the name. For a period in the 1940s the railroad ran a direct train to the Canyon from Los Angeles under the same name.

Though the Canyon depths are not visible from the tracks or the depot, they are only a wink away. El Tovar's front porch offers the closest view. To get there, walk through the west end of the station and up the concrete steps to the front entrance of El Tovar. After taking in the majestic view, look straight down toward the bottom of the Canyon where several hiking trails converge under a cluster of green cottonwood trees. This site is Indian Gardens. When Congress in 1898 authorized the building of the Canyon railroad, Indian Gardens, 4.5 miles down, was its intended terminus – a feat thankfully not achieved.

EPILOGUE

The Canyon railroad offers the prospect of preserving the Canyon's pristine beauty from the increasing threats to its environment from automobiles, congestion, pollution, and mankind itself. It has the potential to reduce automobile congestion at peak season by as many as 4,000 cars daily. It offers the special prospect of returning the Canyon to the safety of nature away from the predations of its one and only natural enemy, mankind. Edward Abbey's words are fitting:

"*It is not enough to describe the world of nature; the point is to preserve it. It is not enough to paint, photograph, or even to understand the American West; the point is to save it. It is not enough to admire or love the Colorado Plateau region; the point is to defend it from its enemies. What we need are heroes and heroines--about a million of them--willing and able to fight for the health of the land and its native inhabitants.... Think of your children. Of their children. Of the hawks, buzzards, lizards, bear. Save a little room and time for the free play of the human spirit and the wild play of the animal kingdom.*"

"*I can think of no better place to draw that line in words of flame, in deeds of conviction--than around the red rock, the sunburnt canyons, the lonesome junipers and the solitary mountain lion of the Colorado Plateau.*" Edward Abbey, Blessed by Light: Visions of the Colorado Plateau. (1986)

BIBLIOGRAPHY

Especially helpful to research on the railroad is the Kaibab National Forest's "Recreation Opportunity Guide," for which I thank archaeologist Teri Cleeland. "Spike" Way's *Summary of Travel to the Grand Canyon* offers helpful historical data on the stage routes and early days of the railroad, as does Al Richmond's book *Cowboys, Miners, Presidents and Kings; The Story of the Grand Canyon Railway*. The October 1989 issue of *The Passenger Train Journal* has an account by Charles Sanno on the railroad's early history. Historical accounts of Flagstaff's involvement with the railroad can be found in Platt Cline's *They Came to the Mountain* and, for Williams, in James Fuchs' essay entitled "A History of Williams, Arizona." Charles Merriam's own books are excellent explanations of his "life zone" theory. *The Williams News* provides excellent current coverage of all railroad events as it has since its origin. There are numerous works on vulcanism but nothing, in my opinion, to match the graphic depictions at the Museum of Northern Arizona in Flagstaff. As to the Canyon, there are hundreds of books, of course—but it speaks well for itself.

About the Author

Rudy J. Gerber's love of trains began in his hometown of St. Louis, Missouri. Since then he has been a college professor, lawyer, writer, and explorer of western canyons. He is currently a judge on the Arizona Court of Appeals. Much of this book was written at his rustic cabin near Williams, where the wail of train whistles can be heard echoing off the mountains.

Map from the Santa Fe timetable circa 1909 showing the route of the railroad from Williams to the Grand Canyon.